Merry Christmas!
Enjoy!
We love you,
LeRoy + Renie 12/25/02

A Southern Palate

Contemporary Seasonal Southern Cuisine
from the Purple Parrot Café and Crescent City Grill

by Robert St. John

with artwork by Wyatt Waters

DIFFERENT DRUMMER PRESS   HATTIESBURG

Preceding pages

Slices of Life

One of the great mysteries of
life is that watermelon tastes
even sweeter when sprinkled
with salt.

Learning
by Ample Eggs

I wanted to pay homage to the
educational benefits of Betty
Crocker and Martha White
at once with this still life. I
don't think the Clabber girl
had a name.

Page 146

The 15-Cent Coke

Brent's Drug Store still serves
up this beverage to customers
in tiny Coke glasses that
remind me of the toy beverage
dispensers from Sears
catalogs. But this is the
real thing.

ISBN 0-9721972-0-6

Printed in China by C&C Offset Printing
Designed and produced by John Langston

All artworks reproduced in *A Southern Palate* are from
the collection of the artist except as follows:

Have Your Cake and Eat It too, page 128
Collection of Frank Grillo and John Morris

The 15-Cent Coke, page 146
Collection of Sherry Lucas

Another Roadside Attraction, page 25
Cheaper by the Dozen, page 142
Collection of Dr. William and Ceci Smith

I Think I Can! I Think I Can! page 16
Collection of Dr. and Mrs. David Boatright

To view more of Wyatt's work visit
WyattWaters.com
and
Wyatt Waters Gallery
306 Jefferson Street
Clinton, MS 39056
(601) 925-8115

FOR JILL

My Love

My Rock

My Inspiration

Acknowledgments

I would like to thank the people who helped to put this book together:

Wyatt Waters, artist, friend, and fellow Beatles enthusiast for his beautiful artwork and creative captions for his paintings.

Bill Dunlap for his excitement, encouragement, and inspirational enthusiasm.

John Langston, book producer, for his artistic vision, knowledge, and patience.

Clint Taylor, friend, business partner, and Purple Parrot general manager for taking care of our company while I took extra time to complete this project.

Linda Nance, for her assistance in recipe testing and stock info.

Cathy Creel, for a year's worth of recipe typing, re-typing, revising, and re-typing again.

Jill, for being my best friend, my sounding board, a dedicated restaurateur's wife, and the most amazing mother in the world.

Frances Karnes, for lighting a fire under my rump.

John Evans, for his wise counsel.

Mom for being a constant example of how to persevere.

And all of the restaurant customers and column readers over the years.

• • •

Many recipes in this book call for Crescent City Grill Hot Sauce or Crescent City Grill Cayenne and Garlic Sauce. Theses sauces may be purchased in any of our restaurants or on our website **www.nsrg.com.** Tabasco, Louisiana Hot Sauce, or your favorite pepper sauce may be substituted in any of the recipes in this book.

Crescent City Grill Creole Seasoning and other dry seasonings are also available in our restaurants or on the website. You may substitute your favorite commercial seasoning if our products are not readily available.

Cottonseed oil is also available in our restaurants or on the website. Cottonseed oil is one of the best oils for use in salad dressings, sautéing and frying and is one of the few oils considered acceptable for reducing saturated fat intake. Cottonseed oil is among the most unsaturated oils. It has a 2:1 ratio of polyunsaturated to saturated fatty acids. Its light, non oily consistency and high smoke point make it most desirable for cooking stir-fry and other oriental dishes, as well as for frying fish. If cottonseed oil is not available in your area, substitute any mild-flavored vegetable-based oil.

Feel free to substitute ingredients and change cooking methods in all of these recipes. None is written in stone. If you don't have a specific ingredient, substitute something close. If you made the wrong choice you will know soon enough. There are no absolutes in this book, and the only law in cooking is to have fun.

Boy-Girl Relationships

The original "happy meal" idea was formed at the Shoney's restaurant chain. This was once a Western Auto store where I bought my first paint. Today, known as Dr. Evil's getaway rocket, it holds a hamburger like a fast food Statue of Liberty.

Many Are Called but Few Are Chosen
or Why Wyatt Paints
with What Robert Brings to a Boil

Consider, if you will, the case of Robert St. John, Wyatt Waters, and their collaborative enterprise, *A Southern Palate*.

What, pray tell, are we to make of these two men—highly civilized, well-spoken, genteel, and mannered sons of the South with impeccable credentials of place, family, education, manhood, and early exposure to religion—who confound polite society by choosing the unsanctified commercial kitchen and painter's studio for their life's work? They might have become lawyers, football coaches, or used car salesmen.

Sigmund Freud would certainly have had a field day with this duo. Take, for example, Robert St. John's recollection of the giddiness he felt as a five-year-old when he found an Easy Bake Oven under his Christmas tree.

The Father of Psychobabble would find equally compelling Mr. Waters's childhood epiphany. Wyatt was never quite the same after helping his mother transform their kitchen floor into simulated linoleum, employing abstract expressionist techniques and enamel paint from the Western Auto store. (The materials and methods preferred by Jackson Pollock, as it were.)

As revealing as these youthful confessions might appear, we can, in our quest for enlightenment, dispense with old Sigmund's pseudo-scientific approach. It just doesn't apply, and here's why.

The central conundrum of psychoanalysis is the question of identity—"Who am I?" It is a given that every child growing up in the American South, by the time he or she is old enough to get to and out the door, has been told countless times, "Now, you remember who you are." So, with the answer indelibly imprinted on their young minds, the question seldom comes up.

A more obvious explanation may be as simple as the coincidence of their assigned surnames—*St. John* and *Waters*. I once knew a podiatrist named Horace *Foote*, a dentist called *Gum*, and a proctologist with the exquisite moniker of *Butts*. The sculptor David *Smith* forged modern masterpieces from iron and steel, and from my friend Bill *Hair* you can get a shampoo, snip, and set in a New York minute. Catch my drift?

While this "name is fate" paradigm is hardly foolproof, it surely follows that a *St. John*

Blind Lemon Catfish

Whiskers is the name of this 80 lb. cat from a breeding farm in Meridian. After painting the celebrity, I was invited to feed her some fish and pet her. I will never eat catfish without thinking of this again.

would end up in the ministry, nurturing the spirit, pressing the flesh, and passing the collection plate while tirelessly proselytizing to faithful, heretic, and infidel alike. Preaching, come to think of it, is exactly what the Right Reverend Robert does all day long from the secular pulpit of his restaurants, The Purple Parrot, Mahogany Bar, and Crescent City Grill in Hattiesburg, Mississippi.

One dares to improve on the Lord's work at his own peril, but it's not much of a stretch to imagine Brother St. John catering the Sermon on the Mount. I suspect the loaves and fishes would stay on the menu with the addition of plenty of garnish and a garlic and holy basil infused olive oil drizzled over the ever-abundant staff of life. How about a crabmeat, crawfish, and andouille sauce for those miraculous fishes, served with a chilled Sea of Galilee Chardonnay? Such a blessed feast should make the Promised Land seem . . . well, all the more so.

Wyatt Waters's career options might seem similarly predestined. As Jesus turned water into wine, so Mississippi's early Scots-Irish settlers became adept at turning water into contraband whiskey, with the help of a little corn and sugar. However, Wyatt's half dozen years spent earning two degrees from Mississippi College, that bastion of Southern Baptistism, would have squeezed the liquor intent out of that great distiller, Lem Motlow—Jack Daniel's founder, for the uninformed. The divining rod business has faltered since Ross Barnett turned the Pearl River into a reservoir. So, what's left is the road less taken.

Somewhere in our dim memory is that initial image-maker who first applied his muddy handprint to the wall of the cave and, stepping back to admire it, uttered the equivalent of, "Oh, yeah. That'll do." This prehistoric ancestor's genes are manifest in Wyatt Waters, who wanted to be an artist well before he knew what one was.

Our beloved South is experiencing a cultural renaissance. Visual artists are finally taking their place alongside our phalanx of fine writers. The southern chef is suddenly someone to be reckoned with. Like morels after a spring rain, they both are popping up in the most unexpected places, and *hallelujah*, they no longer have to leave home to arrive professionally.

These are the uncharted waters in which we find our two artists, working at the height of their powers and choosing to subjugate pride, ego, and self-aggrandizement for the better good of an ambitious collaborative endeavor. And what holds this all together? Water. Two molecules of hydrogen and one of oxygen.

Wyatt's very name is the plural of H_2O. So it is fitting that watercolor, the most demanding, unforgiving, humbling, and ultimately rewarding way to make a painting, would be his method of choice. One masterful picture after another flows from his brush, each vibrating with color, rich in narrative, and layered with meaning. The caliber of his work places him squarely in the grand tradition of American watercolor that includes such immortals as Winslow Homer and John Singer Sargent, and closer to home, Walter Anderson and William Hollingsworth. Wyatt is a prolific and prodigious painter who enjoys a high percentage of success in a medium whose incredible rate of attrition is matched only by that of the restaurant business.

Robert St. John's kitchen wizardry has been widely appreciated and duly celebrated. His stated philosophy "serious food should never be taken too seriously" belies the fact that his unbridled joy in cooking is predicated on an inherent genius—a genius not only for invention, preparation, and presentation, but for recognition of the potential of this burgeoning food phenomenon and the good sense to do something about it.

As far as water and Robert are concerned . . . well, both he and his biblical namesake were baptized in it. As a teetotaler, he drinks gallons of it, and it's for damned sure you can't do much in the way of cooking without it. So there.

We can muse until the milk clabbers about the how and why of Robert St. John's jump from Easy Bake Oven to Viking Industrial Range, and Wyatt Waters's climb up from the kitchen floor to the painter's easel. But in the end, *A Southern Palate* is testament to their journey of faith, good will, and discovery. Their God given talents, hard work, and risks have been rewarded, and so have we . . . with this sumptuous book that, in addition to being a fount of knowledge and a visual treat, is almost good enough to eat.

Bill Dunlap
MCLEAN, VIRGINIA
SPRING 2002

The Man with Kaleidoscope Eyes

If only I could see the world through Wyatt Waters's eyes.

Working from a true southern palette, Wyatt sees colors and images that I never knew existed. Outdoors, if I happen across a pine stump I see an uninteresting piece of brown and green wood. Wyatt sees the same stump and uses it as an opportunity to set down a brilliant explosion of colors—deep-forest greens, milk chocolate, mocha, pink, lavender, and cobalt blue. His palette is as diverse as the state in which he lives.

Wyatt's eyes can detect the simple beauty and intricacies mere mortals miss—an elaborately burled strip of wood in the floor of an auditorium or a snakelike plant with geometric branches, items in which I see no splendor. That is, until he paints them.

Wyatt leaves the photography to photographers. Observed color is the ultimate goal. Preferring to work on location instead of in a studio or from a photograph, he braves the often brutal Mississippi elements to realize the expressive color achieved only when subject and observer interact in person and as one.

Nothing in Wyatt's world goes unnoticed. While working on this book, the two of us spent countless hours in my car. I often sat in awe watching the mental wheels turn in his mind as he gazed through the windshield in search of his next subject. On a road I travel daily, Wyatt would inevitably point out theretofore unseen details in the everyday landscape. They were items I never would have noticed; now subjects sure to end up on an 11" x 15" sheet of handmade 140 lb. D'Arches bright white rough-finish paper.

He sees beauty in the ordinary. In his second book, *Painting Home*, Wyatt traveled Mississippi from border to border, painting the local landmarks and institutions that have canonized each community. To capture the feel of Hattiesburg, my hometown, most artists choose the Victorian-era McLeod House on Main Street, the willow-draped bridge at Lake Byron or the *verde*-domed Administration building at the University of Southern Mississippi, fine landmarks all. Not Wyatt. He chose to paint the then-defunct Beverly Drive-In Theater and the now-defunct California Sandwich Shop. Less official, but better choices. And in their way deep-rooted institutions with character, personality, and history.

The choices are not premeditated and deliberate. They are made using instinct, intuition, and a deep sense of place. While traveling he will slam on brakes in an instant and pull the car over to study a situation that has caught his eye. Then from the backseat appears a rickety, worn, and paint-stained easel. The artist is in.

The easel is not much to look at, one he made at home using scrap wood and spare

Food Coloring

Small children often see my palette and remark that I paint with rainbows. The palate and the palette overlap—"What does blue taste like?"

hardware. Conversely, the masterworks created on it make use of time-honed skills and innate artistry.

Like the subjects he chooses, Wyatt's own character, personality, and sense of place fuel his artistry. He is not only Mississippi's greatest living watercolorist; he is a raconteur for the entire South. For him, painting exists as a method by which to explore the mysteries and complexities of everyday life. Consider the mysteries solved.

Wyatt, like me, loves music. We have an ongoing feud as to who is the foremost expert on the Beatles (it's me). On one point, we both agree—the Fab Four changed the world's musical landscape forever. In 1967, during one of the most creative periods ever experienced by an artist or group of artists, the Beatles recorded the *Sgt. Pepper's Lonely Hearts Club Band* album. It revolutionized the way we listen to and visualize popular music.

On *Sgt. Pepper,* John Lennon painted vivid musical images of marmalade skies, tangerine trees, cellophane flowers of yellow and green, and a girl with kaleidoscope eyes. That is Wyatt's world.

Thirty-five years later, and in the middle of a similar Sgt. Pepper period—his Sgt. Pepper period—Wyatt is revolutionizing the way we look at Mississippi, at our neighbors, and at ourselves.

Wyatt Waters is truly the man with kaleidoscope eyes.

A Southern Palate

Shrimp Cocktail

I once overheard a woman approach a bar and ask for "anything with an umbrella in it."

Appetizers

Shiitake Shrimp over Fried Andouille Cheese Grits

Fried Green Tomatoes

Crabmeat Holleman

Crabmeat Martini

Crawfish Pizza

Creole Cheese Fritters

Black-eyed Pea Cakes with Crab Pico de Gallo

Duck Confit Nachos

Mushroom Ravioli

Crawfish Quesadillas

Smoked Duck Spring Rolls

Crawfish Madeline

Shiitake Shrimp over Fried Andouille Cheese Grits

Fried Andouille Cheese Grit Triangles

Andouille Cheese Grits (p.95), chilled and cut into 1½-inch triangles

1 cup **Seasoned Flour (p. 107)**

1 cup **Eggwash (p. 107)**

1 cup seasoned breadcrumbs

cottonseed oil for frying

Dip cheese grit triangles in seasoned flour, then in eggwash, then in seasoned breadcrumbs. Heat cottonseed oil to 350° in a heavy skillet. Gently place the breaded triangles in the hot oil and cook on both sides until golden. Drain triangles on paper towels and hold them in a warm oven while you prepare the topping.

Topping

18 large shrimp, peeled and deveined

1 tablespoon Crescent City Grill Creole Seasoning

2 ounces **Clarified Butter (p. 107)**

1½ cups shiitake mushrooms, thinly sliced

6 cloves roasted garlic

½ cup **Caramelized Onions (p. 101)**

¾ cup **Roasted Red Bell Pepper (p. 105)**, julienned (about one small pepper)

3 ounces white wine

1½ cups **Lemon Meuniere (p. 122)**

¼ cup fresh parsley, chopped fine

¼ cup green onion, thinly sliced

In a large skillet, heat clarified butter over medium high heat. Season the shrimp with the creole seasoning and sauté for 3–4 minutes. Add the shiitakes and cook for 3–4 more minutes. Add the roasted peppers, garlic, and onion and deglaze with the white wine. Allow the wine to reduce and remove from heat. Add the lemon meuniere. Remove grits from warm oven and place one triangle on each serving dish. Place 3 shrimp on each plate and then spoon sauce evenly over the grits. Garnish with chopped parsley and green onions.

Yield: 6 servings

Fried Green Tomatoes

18 green tomato slices (3–4 large green tomatoes)
1½ cups **Seasoned Flour (p.107)**
1½ cups **Eggwash (p. 107)**
1½ cups breadcrumbs
cottonseed oil for frying

Dip tomato into flour, then in eggwash, then lightly coat with breadcrumbs. Heat oil to 350°. Fry until golden brown. Drain on paper towels and hold in a warm oven at 175°.

Topping

3 ounces **Clarified Butter (p. 107)**
1½ cups mushrooms, sliced (shiitake, button, or porto-
    bello, or a mixture)
⅓ cup red peppers, small dice
⅓ cup green peppers, small dice
1 tablespoon garlic, minced
½ pound jumbo lump crabmeat, picked clean
2 ounces red wine
¾ cup **Crescent City Grill Creole Sauce (p. 110)**
¼ teaspoon salt
1½ cups **Beurre Blanc (p. 112)**
¼ cup fresh parsley, chopped
¼ cup fresh chives, chopped

Heat butter in a large skillet over medium high heat and sauté mushrooms. Cook for 3–4 minutes, then add garlic and diced peppers. Continue to cook 3–5 more minutes. Add creole sauce. Add crabmeat and deglaze with red wine. Let the wine reduce until almost evaporated. Remove from heat and add salt, parsley, and beurre blanc. On 6 serving dishes, place a fried green tomato slice and top it with a small amount of mixture, then another layer of fried tomato and crab mixture. Finally, one last tomato slice and top it off with remaining mixture. Garnish with freshly chopped chives and serve immediately.

Yield: 6 servings

"Never eat more than you can lift."—Miss Piggy

Crabmeat Holleman

Crabmeat Martini

½ cup Hellman's Mayonnaise

2 egg yolks

1 teaspoon Worcestershire

1 teaspoon Crescent City Grill Cayenne and Garlic Sauce

1 tablespoon sherry

1 tablespoon creole mustard

1 tablespoon lemon juice

1 teaspoon Crescent City Grill Creole Seasoning

⅓ cup green bell peppers, small dice

⅓ cup red bell peppers, small dice

1 pound jumbo lump crabmeat

½ pound backfin crabmeat

2 8–ounce wheels or wedges of Brie (remove rind and cut into ½ inch cubes)

6 tablespoons seasoned breadcrumbs

Preheat oven to 375°. Combine mayonnaise, egg yolks, Worcestershire, cayenne and garlic sauce, sherry, creole mustard, lemon juice, and creole seasoning; mix well with a wire whisk. Stir in peppers. Gently fold crabmeat into liquid mixture, being sure not to break up lumps. Place a layer of crabmeat mix in ovenproof ramekin or scallop shells, then 2 cubes of Brie and another layer of crab. Top with seasoned breadcrumbs and bake for 10–22 minutes, until mixture bubbles and crumbs are brown. Garnish with chopped parsley.

Yield: 8 servings

¼ red onion, small dice

1 pound jumbo lump crabmeat (gently picked of all shell)

⅔ cup lemon-flavored oil

2 tablespoons olive oil (not extra virgin)

1½ teaspoons Absolut Citron Vodka (optional)

½ cup white balsamic vinegar

¼ cup ice cold water

1 teaspoon salt

1 teaspoon freshly ground black pepper

1 teaspoon Crescent City Grill Cayenne and Garlic Sauce

2 teaspoons cilantro

2 teaspoons parsley

In a large mixing bowl, combine all ingredients and gently toss with a rubber spatula, being careful not to break up any of the lumps of crabmeat. Cover and store in refrigerator 12 hours (tossing every hour or so) to let flavors marry. Gently toss (or turn over) just before serving, as the lemon vinaigrette will separate. Divide crabmeat mixture among 4 lettuce-lined martini glasses. Drizzle excess vinaigrette over the crabmeat to wet the lettuce. Garnish with a skewered olive for a light and cool first course or double the recipe and serve on a lettuce-lined plate for a luncheon salad. Serve the leftovers in a decorative bowl on the coffee table to be spooned atop your favorite cracker as an hors d'oeuvre.

Yield: 6 servings, appetizers; 4 servings, salad

Crawfish Pizza

1 tablespoon olive oil
½ cup green bell peppers, chopped fine
½ cup yellow onion, chopped fine
½ cup green onion, chopped fine
1 tablespoon garlic, minced
2 teaspoons Crescent City Grill Creole Seasoning
¾ pound crawfish tail meat, cooked and in whole pieces
6 **Pizza Crusts (p. 106)**
1½ cups **Basil Tapenade (p. 119)**
1½ cups mozzarella cheese, shredded
1 cup pepper jack cheese, shredded
½ cup Parmesan cheese, freshly grated

In a large skillet, heat olive oil over medium heat. Sauté peppers, onion, and garlic until slightly tender. Add creole seasoning and crawfish. Remove from heat and let cool slightly (may be prepared a day in advance). Preheat oven to 450°. Arrange pizza crusts on a baking sheet. Spread the basil tapenade evenly on top of each pizza crust. Distribute the crawfish mixture over the tapenade and top with the mozzarella cheese. Top with pepper jack cheese and Parmesan. Bake for 12–14 minutes, until crust is golden brown and all cheese has melted. Remove from the oven and let rest for 3–4 minutes before cutting.

Yield: 6 pizzas

Creole Cheese Fritters

¾ cup Parmesan cheese, freshly grated
3 eggs
¼ cup parsley, chopped fine
¼ cup green onions, medium dice
¼ cup horseradish
¼ cup sour cream
1½ tablespoons garlic, minced
1 tablespoon Crescent City Grill Creole Seasoning
¼ teaspoon red pepper, crushed
1 cup flour
½ tablespoon Crescent City Grill Cayenne and Garlic Sauce
10 ounces pepper jack cheese, grated
6 ounces mozzarella cheese, grated
6 ounces cheddar cheese, grated
cottonseed oil for frying
Comeback Sauce (p. 119)

Place Parmesan cheese, eggs, parsley, onions, horseradish, sour cream, garlic, creole seasoning, red pepper, flour, and cayenne and garlic sauce in an electric mixer and combine at medium speed. Add the 3 cheeses and continue mixing until well blended.

Heat cottonseed oil to 350° in a cast iron skillet. Drop golf ball-size spoonfuls of cheese fritter mixture into hot oil, making sure not to cook too many at once.

Serve with comeback sauce for dipping.
Yield: 24–30

"We may live without poetry, music, and art; We may live without conscience, and live without heart; We may live without friends; We may live without books; But civilized man cannot live without cooks."—'Lucile' Owen Meredith

Cold Drinks

Southerners love soft drinks. We call them cold drinks. Mississippi summers require multiple daily doses of cold drinks. The sweeter the cold drink, the better. And, no matter what the cold drink is—7-Up, Mountain Dew, or a Barq's Root Beer—we call it "Coke."

The best Cokes in the world are still served in the little 8-ounce glass bottles. I don't know what it is about that little bottle, but Coke tastes better in it. My favorite diners and small cafes still serve Cokes in 8-ounce bottles.

I remember the day I drank my first Mountain Dew. I don't remember many firsts. But I do remember my first beer, a Miller pony, and my first Mountain Dew. It was sometime in the mid-1960s. My uncle Dwight and I were walking along the railroad tracks, a few blocks from my grandmother's house. We were putting pennies down on the railroad track and watching the train flatten them.

That first Mountain Dew was in a tall, 10-ounce green glass bottle with a hillbilly on it. The hillbilly was barefooted and holding a moonshine jug with "Mountain Dew" written on the side. The cork was shooting out of the jug right through his Jed Clampett-style hat.

The bottle had the worst tag line in the history of tag lines: "It'll tickle yore innards!"

A Madison Avenue northerner must have come up with this advertising campaign. The stereotypical barefooted hillbilly was saying "Ya-hoo," as all southerners must do from time to time, for no apparent reason.

Why, I can't get through a day without one or two loud and hearty "Ya-hoo's!"

"We enjoyed our fish today, Mr. St. John."

"Ya-hoo!" I say. "And y'all come back now, you hear. Has anyone seen my shoes?"

The barefooted Mountain Dew hillbilly looked like one of the characters out of *Deliverance.* Some of the logos had the barefooted hillbilly chasing a nosey revenuer down the hill, with his double-barreled shotgun. The revenuer was running in front of an outhouse (which is where I always run when the revenuers are after me).

I blame the Mountain Dew hillbilly, along with Jethro Bodine, Gomer Pyle, and *Deliverance* for perpetuating the barefooted-southern-redneck myth. Every southerner

Many Happy Returns

I collected many small, raised-letter bottles of coke before they quit making them. The others were collected under houses and in junk piles during painting trips. A little food coloring, a little water, and Presto!—a new Sunrise.

I know wears shoes. We might not wear socks, but we all wear shoes—all of us except those people they dig up to do UFO-sighting interviews on national TV.

Today, Mountain Dew is targeting the "extreme" market. These new advertisements feature young, adventurous males mountain biking and snowboarding. Just once, I would like to see that old barefooted Mountain Dew hillbilly from the sixties come running into one of the new extreme commercials and chase all of those testosterone-fueled youths off the mountain with his double-barreled shotgun.

Brett Favre's life-size picture is on the Mountain Dew machine at my neighborhood grocery store. His face was on some Mountain Dew cans, too. Brett is a good ol' South Mississippi boy. He lives in my town. And I know for a fact that he wears shoes everywhere he goes.

Brett Favre has enough money to buy the whole Mountain Dew factory. Maybe he will buy it and make me the advertising director. I would get rid of all traces of the barefooted hillbilly, and insert a preppy Yale law student (with loafers) in his place. Instead of "Ya-hoo!" he could be saying "You guys!" Maybe he could chase mountain bikers and snowboarders down the mountain with a polo stick. We would change the name from Mountain Dew to Yankee Pop. Now that would tickle my innards.

I bought a Mountain Dew today. It was in a plastic bottle. The bottle had a baseball player, not a barefooted hillbilly, on the side of the bottle. The baseball player wasn't saying anything. He was swinging a bat. I couldn't tell if he was a southern baseball player or not—I couldn't see his feet.

Black-Eyed Pea Cakes with Crab Pico di Gallo

3 cups black-eyed peas, cooked
½ cup green onion, finely sliced
⅓ cup red peppers, small dice
1 egg
½ teaspoon cumin
1 teaspoon Crescent City Grill Creole Seasoning
¼ cup Romano cheese, shredded
1 cup breadcrumbs, finely ground
½ cup **Seasoned Flour (p. 107)**
2–3 tablespoons **Clarified Butter (p. 107)**
Crab Pico di Gallo
1 cup **Seafood Remoulade (p. 118)**
¼ cup cilantro, chopped

With your hands or a potato masher, smash the black-eyed peas, leaving a few pieces whole. Add green onion, red pepper, spices, and egg. Mix thoroughly. Add cheese and breadcrumbs and mix well. Divide the mix into 12 1½-inch balls. Flatten balls to 2 inches in diameter and about ½ inch thick. This may be done a day ahead of time, covered and stored in the refrigerator.

To cook the cakes, preheat oven to 425°. Heat butter over medium high heat in a large skillet. Lightly dust both sides of the cakes with seasoned flour and place them in the skillet to brown. Leave enough room between cakes to be able to flip them over. When cakes are brown on both sides, place them on a baking sheet and put them in the oven for 7 minutes, or until heated through.

Arrange 2 cakes on each serving dish so that one is flat and one is resting at an angle against the flat one. Divide the pico di gallo evenly over the cakes. Using a squirt bottle, garnish the plate with seafood remoulade. Sprinkle with freshly chopped cilantro and serve hot.

Crab Pico di Gallo

1½ cups tomato, seeds removed and small dice
¼ cup yellow onion, small dice
1½ tablespoons jalapeño pepper, seeds removed and small dice
3 tablespoons lime juice
1 tablespoon white vinegar
2 teaspoons salt
⅓ cup cilantro, chopped
½ pound jumbo lump crabmeat (backfin meat will also work for this recipe)

Mix all ingredients and allow to marinate in the refrigerator, gently stirring occasionally for 2–4 hours prior to serving.
  Yield: 6 servings

"Not all chemicals are bad. Without chemicals such as hydrogen and oxygen, for example, there would be no way to make water, a vital ingredient in beer."
—Dave Barry

Duck Confit Nachos

"To eat well in England
you should have breakfast
three times a day."
—W. Somerset Maugham

2 tablespoons **Clarified Butter (p. 107)**
½ cup yellow onion, minced
¼ cup red peppers, finely diced
¼ cup green peppers, finely diced
2 tablespoons garlic, minced
2 teaspoons Crescent City Grill Creole Seasoning
1 cup duck confit, small dice
1½ cups pepper jack cheese, finely grated
1 large sweet potato, thinly sliced
cottonseed oil for frying
¼ cup fresh chives, chopped

In a medium skillet, heat the clarified butter over medium heat. Add onions and peppers and sauté until soft. Add the garlic and creole seasoning. Cook for an additional 2 minutes. Remove skillet from the heat. Transfer mix into mixing bowl and refrigerate until cool. Once the mixture is cool, add the duck confit and cheese and mix it thoroughly. This step may be done a day in advance.

Peel sweet potato and slice into very thin slices. Heat cottonseed oil to 340° in a heavy skillet. Drop several chips at a time and fry until crispy and bright orange. Don't fry too many at a time; you will need to be able to pull them out quickly. This step may be done 30 minutes to an hour ahead of serving time. Drain chips on paper towels to remove excess oil.

Preheat oven to 400° and arrange chips on a baking sheet. Top with one heaping tablespoon of the duck mixture and place in the oven. Bake until cheese is melted and mixture is warm. Garnish with fresh chopped chives.

Duck Confit

½ pound duck meat (either leg or breast), cut into medium to large strips
1½ cups bacon fat
1 tablespoon kosher salt
1 tablespoon fresh ground black pepper
1 sprig fresh thyme
1 bay leaf
1 clove garlic, smashed

Place a cooling rack on baking sheet. Generously season the duck with the salt and black pepper. Place the duck on the cooling rack and refrigerate for 4–6 hours. Preheat the oven to 225°. In a small ovenproof baking dish, melt the bacon fat. Place the duck meat in the warm, but not hot, bacon fat, making sure it is completely submerged. Add the thyme, bay leaf, and garlic and cover. Place in the 225° oven. If you are using breast meat, cook for 1½ hours; leg meat will need to cook for 2½ hours. Remove from oven and allow the meat to cool down for 20 minutes while still in bacon fat. Remove from bacon fat, and it is now ready for the duck confit nacho recipe. This step may be done one day in advance. If so, hold the cooked duck in the bacon fat. (It must be completely covered in the fat.)

Yield: 6–8 servings as a passed appetizer

Mushroom Ravioli

¼ pound butter, unsalted

6 cups fresh mushrooms (shiitake, portobello, button), very
    fine dice (approximately 2 pounds before chopping)

½ cup shallots, finely minced

1 cup white wine

1½ teaspoons salt

½ teaspoon freshly ground black pepper

1 cup Parmesan cheese, finely grated

1 egg

¾ cup breadcrumbs

½ tablespoon fresh thyme, chopped

1 tablespoon fresh parsley, chopped

1 tablespoon fresh basil, chopped

1 package spring roll wrappers

1 egg + 2 tablespoons water for **Eggwash (p. 107)**

1 recipe of **Tomato and Basil Butter Sauce (p. 112)**

In a large skillet, melt butter over medium high heat. Place mushrooms in the skillet and cook for 3–5 minutes, stirring often. Add garlic, shallots, salt, and pepper and continue to cook for 5 minutes. Add wine and continue to cook until all moisture has evaporated. Place this mixture in a large mixing bowl and allow to cool.

Once the mixture has cooled, add cheese, egg, bread-crumbs, and fresh herbs. Mix thoroughly. To assemble ravioli, place a spring roll wrapper on a flat, dry surface and place balls (4 tablespoons) of the mushroom mixture in the center about 1½ inch from each corner. Brush the exposed surface with eggwash, and top this with another sheet of dough. Press the 2 sheets together and smooth out any air bubbles. Using a 2½-inch circular cookie cutter, cut out each ravioli, making sure the edges are sealed. Place on a dry surface.

Bring 1 gallon of salted water to a slow boil in a large sauce pot. Gently place ravioli in the slowly boiling water. Ravioli are very fragile, rapidly boiling water will cause them to break apart. Cook for 3–4 minutes. Gently spoon the ravioli into a colander and lightly oil them to prevent sticking. Place on serving dishes and top with tomato and basil butter sauce.

Ravioli may be frozen for future use. After you have filled them, place them on a baking sheet lined with wax paper. The ravioli should not touch. You can layer them in between sheets of wax paper. Cover them tightly with plastic wrap and freeze. When you want to use them, leave them out overnight in the refrigerator.

Yield: 36–40 ravioli (8–10 servings as appetizer; 4–6 servings as entrée)

"I feel the end approaching. Quick, bring me my dessert, coffee, and liqueur."
—Brillat-Savarin's great aunt Pierette

Crawfish Quesadillas

"Why, sometimes I've believed as many as six impossible things before breakfast."
—Lewis Carroll

6 16-inch flour tortillas or 12 6-inch tortillas
3 tablespoons butter
1 tablespoon olive oil
¼ cup green bell peppers, chopped fine
¼ cup red bell peppers, chopped fine
1 jalapeño, small dice
½ cup yellow onion, chopped fine
½ cup green onion, chopped fine
1 tablespoon garlic, minced
2 teaspoons Crescent City Grill Creole Seasoning
¾ pound crawfish tail meat, rough chopped
2 tablespoons fresh cilantro, chopped
2 cups jalapeño jack cheese, shredded
sour cream and salsa for serving

Preheat oven to 350°. In a large skillet, heat olive oil and sauté green bell peppers, red bell peppers, jalapeño, yellow onion, green onion, and garlic until tender. Remove from heat and add creole seasoning and crawfish. Allow mixture to cool. Once cooled, add cilantro and cheese. Mix well.

In a large skillet over medium heat, melt a small amount of butter. You will be preparing one tortilla at a time so divide the butter into 6 portions. Place one tortilla in the hot butter and cook until the bottom side becomes a golden brown. Remove and place on a paper towel to drain. Repeat the process with all of the tortillas.

Once you have browned all of the tortillas, spread filling over half of the unbrowned side of the tortilla (about 1¼ cups of filling per quesadilla). Fold the tortilla in half and place quesadillas on baking sheet. If using 6-inch tortillas, you will still brown only one side, then lay one tortilla down, top with filling and place another tortilla on top (browned side up). Place in preheated oven and bake for 10–14 minutes, until cheese has melted and filling is hot.

Yield: 6–10 servings

Smoked Duck Spring Rolls

¾ pound cabbage, finely chopped and blanched
8 ounces ground pork, browned in a skillet and drained
8 ounces duck tenderloins (or breast meat), smoked and rough chopped
⅓ cup mushrooms, sautéed, drained, and chopped fine
3 tablespoons soy sauce
1 tablespoon rice wine
2 teaspoons garlic, minced
1 tablespoon sesame oil
1 teaspoon salt
1 teaspoon pepper
1 package egg roll wraps
cottonseed oil for frying
Spring Roll Sauce (p. 120)

Mix together all ingredients, except the egg roll wraps. To wrap spring rolls follow the instructions on the package of egg roll wrappers, using ¼ cup of the duck mixture for the filling. Roll and seal with beaten egg yolk. Deep fry at 350° until golden brown. Serve with spring roll sauce.

Yield: 10-12 spring rolls

Crawfish Madeline

6 puff pastry shells
2½ cups **Creole Cream Sauce (p. 113)**
½ cup heavy cream
1 pound crawfish tail meat, cooked
¾ cup green onion, sliced
¾ cup Romano or Parmesan cheese, grated
4 tablespoons chives, chopped

Follow the baking instructions on the puff pastry shell box. While shells are baking, bring the creole cream sauce to a simmer over medium high heat in a large skillet. Once it begins to simmer, add heavy cream and crawfish tails. Return to a simmer and allow mixture to cook for 3–4 minutes until it is thoroughly heated. Stir in the green onions and once again bring it up to a simmer. Remove from heat. Place puff pastry shells on serving dishes and evenly divide the mixture over the top of the pastry. Top each one with grated cheese and chives, serve immediately.

Yield: 6 servings

"I'll bet what motivated the British to colonize so much of the world is that they were just looking for a decent meal."
—Martha Harrison

Salads

Purple Parrot Sensation Salad

Grilled Chicken Sensation Salad

Comeback Shrimp Pasta Salad

Sesame-Soy Chicken Salad

Buffalo Chicken Salad

Smoked Tuna Pasta Salad

Seared Salmon Caesar

Café Cobb Salad

Comeback Pasta Salad

Café Salad with Crispy Fried Proscuitto

Roasted Corn and Black Bean Salad

**I Think I Can!
I Think I Can!**

Ball, Mason, Atlas, and Kerr
are all different names for
one thing, canning jars.
What's missing from this
picture? A biscuit, maybe?

Purple Parrot Sensation Salad

"When men reach their sixties and retire, they go to pieces. Women go right on cooking."—Gail Sheehy

6 cups mixed salad greens (2 parts iceberg lettuce, 2 parts romaine lettuce, 1 part spinach)
½ cup Purple Parrot Sensation Dressing
¾ cup Purple Parrot Sensation Cheese Mix

Place salad greens in a mixing bowl and add just enough dressing to wet the greens. Stir the dressing well, as the garlic tends to linger at the bottom of the bowl. Once the greens are dressed, add the cheese mixture and toss well. Place individual portions of the salad on chilled plates and serve immediately.
  Yield: 6 servings

Purple Parrot Sensation Cheese Mix

2 cups Romano cheese, grated
¼ cup bleu cheese, crumbled

Combine ingredients and store in an airtight container.
  Yield: 2¼ cups

Purple Parrot Sensation Dressing

3 tablespoons garlic, minced
½ cup white wine vinegar
½ cup lemon juice, freshly squeezed
⅔ cup olive oil
3½ cups cottonseed oil
2 tablespoons salt, to taste

Combine garlic, vinegar, and lemon juice. Slowly whisk in oils. Add salt.
  Yield: 5 cups

Grilled Chicken Sensation Salad

6 chicken breasts, boneless and skinless
1 tablespoon Crescent City Grill Poultry Seasoning
4 cups green leaf lettuce, chopped
6 cups spring mix (mesclun mix or baby lettuce mix will work)
¼ cup bleu cheese crumbles
¾ cup Romano cheese, grated
1½ cups Purple Parrot Sensation Dressing
1 pint cherry tomatoes
6 cherry peppers

Season chicken with poultry seasoning and grill. Set aside.
  In a food processor, combine the 2 cheeses and pulse until they reach a fine crumble state. Toss half of the cheese with the lettuce and dressing. Arrange lettuces on serving dishes. Cut chicken into long strips and arrange them on top of the salad. Garnish with cherry tomatoes and cherry peppers and sprinkle remaining cheese over top.
  Yield: 6 servings

Comeback Shrimp Pasta Salad

Sesame-Soy Chicken Salad

To prepare shrimp:

3 pounds shrimp

2 gallons water

3 tablespoons crab boil

½ cup garlic

4 bay leaves

¼ cup salt

½ cup lemon juice

Bring all ingredients except shrimp to a boil and simmer for 10–15 minutes. Add shrimp and simmer slowly until shrimp are done (approximately 6 minutes). Drain shrimp and spread out on a cookie sheet. Refrigerate immediately to cool.

To prepare salad:

2½ pounds dry pasta, mixed variety (to equal 6 quarts cooked)

1½ cups celery

1 cup red onion

½ cup green onion

4 large hard-boiled eggs

3 cups **Comeback Sauce (p. 119)**

3 pounds shrimp, boiled, peeled, and deveined

Cook pasta in slightly salted water until tender, then drain. Rinse under cold water until cool. Drain well. Add celery, onion, eggs, comeback sauce, and shrimp and toss. May be prepared 5–6 hours in advance. Serve on a bed of fresh lettuce. If prepared in advance, re-toss pasta just before serving. Garnish with lemon and parsley.

Yield: 10–12 servings

2 pounds fresh spinach, stems removed

6 4-ounce chicken breasts, seasoned, grilled, cubed, and chilled

¾ cup celery

2 carrots, cut on bias and steamed until tender

¾ cup red bell peppers, julienned

1 cantaloupe, peeled and cut into 1-inch cubes

1½ cups **Sesame Soy Dressing**

Stir dressing well. Toss chicken, spinach, celery, cantaloupe, carrots, red peppers, and dressing together in a large mixing bowl or in individual dishes.

Yield: 6 servings

Sesame-Soy Dressing

1 tablespoon dry mustard

½ cup + 2 tablespoons sugar

5 tablespoons soy sauce

½ cup + 2 tablespoons white wine vinegar

1 tablespoon sesame oil

2 cups cottonseed oil

Mix together the mustard, sugar, soy sauce, and vinegar. Slowly add the sesame oil and cottonseed oil using a wire whisk. Refrigerate for two hours and stir well before serving.

Yield: 1 quart

"Cookery is become an art, a noble science; cooks are gentlemen."—Robert Burton

Thirty Cooking Tips for Beginners

1. Cook only what you like to eat.
2. If a recipe looks too hard, cook it anyway; it won't be as hard next time.
3. Have fun.
4. If you screw up, so what—it's only food. Cook it again or move on.
5. It makes no difference how many ingredients are in a recipe, procedure is where skill and experience are needed.
6. Master the art of the "perfect scrambled egg."
7. Never experiment with an untested recipe when you are cooking for guests.
8. If your guests are close friends, experiment all day long.
9. Don't be afraid to improvise—recipes are not laws.
10. Have fun.
11. Once a week, experiment in your kitchen, on your own, with ingredients and procedures you haven't used before.
12. Eat only what you like to cook.
13. Tuna casserole sucks, don't ever cook it.
14. Keep cooking until you have mastered fried chicken and mashed potatoes. When you can cook them better than anyone else, move on.
15. Return to fried chicken and mashed potatoes often.
16. Steamed broccoli will stink up your kitchen.
17. Cook with your friends whenever you can (make them chop the onions).
18. Clean as you go.
19. Taste as you go.
20. Have fun.
21. If you have friends who are good cooks, go to their house and cook with them (they'll probably make you chop the onions).
22. If you have children, cook with them. If you don't, borrow someone else's children and cook with them.

The Midnight Snack

When the kitchen lights are off and one sneaks in to have a bite to eat, the glow of the refrigerator makes even the tiniest morsel comfort food.

23. Never cook a hard-boiled egg in a microwave.
24. Don't be afraid to substitute ingredients. You will know very quickly if you chose the wrong substitute (and you probably won't make the same mistake twice).
25. Always make biscuits from scratch.
26. Shop at the farmers' market.
27. Learn how to use herbs and seasonings with the proper "touch." When seasoning food, more is never better.
28. Teach yourself how to make cakes from scratch.
29. Learn how to make the perfect piecrust.
30. Always have fun!

Buffalo Chicken Salad

24 chicken tenders, about 2–2½ pounds
1 cup whipping cream
1 cup buttermilk
4 eggs
2 tablespoons Crescent City Grill Creole Seasoning
2 teaspoons salt
2 cups **Seasoned Flour (p. 107)**
cottonseed oil for frying
5 cups romaine lettuce, chopped
5 cups green leaf lettuce, chopped
1 cup bleu cheese crumbles
2 carrots, peeled and sliced thinly on a bias, then blanched*
2 cups bleu cheese dressing
1½ cups Crescent City Grill Hot Sauce
½ cup honey
2 tablespoons margarine, melted

Mix the whipping cream, buttermilk, eggs, creole seasoning, and salt. Add the chicken and marinate overnight, or for at least 8 hours.

Chill the lettuces, bleu cheese, blanched carrots, and dressing for the salad.

To make the buffalo sauce, mix together the hot sauce, honey, and melted margarine and set aside.

In a large heavy-duty skillet, heat to 350° enough cottonseed oil to fry chicken tenders. Drain the marinade from the chicken tenders and coat them generously with the seasoned flour. Fry the tenders a few at a time depending on the size of the skillet. They will take about 7–9 minutes to cook. Remove them from the oil and drain on paper towels. If it is necessary to prepare several batches of the chicken tenders, place the cooked tenders in the oven on low heat to hold them until you have cooked all of the chicken.

Once the chicken is cooked, assemble the salad, mixing the dressing with the lettuces and half the bleu cheese crumbles. Divide the salad into serving dishes.

In a large bowl, toss the tenders with the buffalo sauce. Arrange the tenders around the outside of the salad and top each salad with a few slices of the blanched carrot and remaining bleu cheese crumbles.

* To blanch carrots, bring a large amount of slightly salted water to a rapid boil. Have an ice bath ready. Place carrots in boiling water and cook for 1½ minutes, until they become slightly flexible. They should still have some crunch in them. Remove them from the boiling water and plunge them into the ice water to stop the cooking process. Drain when cooled. You can do this step hours in advance.

Yield: 6 servings

"A stomach that is seldom empty despises common food."
—Horace, Roman lyric poet

Smoked Tuna Pasta Salad

3 pounds fresh tuna (whole loin or thick steaks)
1 cup **Creamy Balsamic Vinaigrette (p. 123)**
2½ pounds dry rotini pasta (to equal 6 quarts cooked)
1½ cups black olives, sliced
1 cup red onion, small dice
1 cup red bell pepper, small dice
1 cup green bell pepper, small dice
2 cups fresh tomatoes, medium dice
3½ cups **Creamy Balsamic Vinaigrette (p. 123)**
1 tablespoon salt
½ tablespoon black pepper
½ cup fresh parsley

Rub the outside of the tuna thoroughly with 1 cup creamy balsamic vinaigrette and allow it to marinate for 2–3 hours. Then using your outdoor grill, smoke the tuna slowly until it reaches medium to medium well doneness. Overcooking will dry out the tuna. Cool and cut into ¾ inch cubes.

Combine tuna with all of the remaining ingredients and mix well. Chill for 2–3 hours before serving. Garnish with fresh parsley.

Yield: 10–12 servings

Seared Salmon Caesar Salad

3–4 tablespoons olive oil or **Clarified Butter (p. 107)**
6 6-ounce portions of salmon
3–4 tablespoons Crescent City Grill Creole Seasoning
12 cups romaine lettuce (about 1½ heads, cut, cleaned, and dried)
2 cups croutons
1½ cups caesar dressing
1 cup grated Parmesan cheese

Preheat oven to 400°. Heat clarified butter in a large skillet or sauté pan on high heat. Butter should be almost to smoking point. Dust salmon steaks or filets with creole seasoning. Sear seasoned salmon in skillet until golden brown and turn to brown on both sides. Do not overload skillet or the salmon will not brown.

Place seared filets on lightly greased baking sheet and place in the oven. Cook to medium, approximately 8–12 minutes; cooking times will vary depending on the thickness of salmon. Toss lettuce with dressing, croutons, and ¾ cup of cheese. Place on serving dish and top with salmon. Garnish with remaining grated cheese.

Yield: 6 servings

Another Roadside Attraction

Behind the zoo is a roadside salesman. His wares are greens, apples, peas, whatever is in season. When I painted him, it was cold and he was boiling peanuts. He was his own advertisement.

Café Cobb Salad

"Cooking is one of the oldest arts and one which has rendered us the most important service in civic life."
—Jean-Anthelme Brillat-Savarin

3 pounds mixed lettuces (mesclun, spring mix)
2 cups bacon bits
5 eggs, hard-boiled and diced or grated
5 cups tomato, diced
5 avocados, diced and tossed with a bit of lemon juice to preserve color
3 pounds chicken, grilled and diced
2 cups green onion
2 cups bleu cheese
2 cups dressing

Toss greens with dressing and place on a large serving dish. Arrange all ingredients in long rows across the entire top surface of the lettuce.

Yield: 6–8 servings

Comeback Pasta Salad

2½ pounds dried rotini (to equal 6 quarts cooked)
1½ cups celery
1 cup red onion
½ cup green onion
4 large hard-boiled eggs
3 cups **Comeback Sauce (p. 119)**

Cook pasta in slightly salted water until al dente. Drain in a colander and rinse under cold water until cool. Drain well. Toss with celery, onion, eggs, and comeback sauce. May be prepared 5–6 hours in advance. Serve on a bed of fresh lettuce. If prepared in advance, re-toss pasta just before serving. Garnish with lemon and parsley.

Yield: 10–12 servings

Café Salad with Crispy Fried Prosciutto

3 cups spring mix baby greens
3 cups green leaf lettuce, chopped
½ cup **Honey-Roasted Nuts (p. 101)**
4 ounces goat cheese, crumbled
¼ pound **Crispy Fried Prosciutto (p. 92)**
1 cup **Raspberry Vinaigrette (p.123)**

Toss lettuces with the raspberry vinaigrette and divide onto serving plates. Top with honey-roasted nuts, goat cheese, and crispy fried prosciutto.

Yield: 6 servings

Roasted Corn and Black Bean Salad

2 cups black beans, cooked and drained
2 cups fresh corn kernels, roasted
1 cup **Tomato Concassee (p. 107)**
½ cup red onion, small dice
2 tablespoons fresh jalapeño, minced
2 tablespoons fresh cilantro, chopped
1 teaspoon cumin
1 teaspoon coriander
2 teaspoons Crescent City Grill Cayenne and Garlic Sauce
Juice from two limes
Salt and pepper to taste

Gently combine all ingredients.

Serve as an accompaniment to seared scallops or blackened shrimp. Or serve as a first-course salad on a bed of lettuce.

Yield: 6-8

"Cooking is at once child's play and adult joy. And cooking done with care is an act of love."—Craig Claiborne

Soups

Purple Parrot Corn and Crab Bisque

Crescent City Grill Seafood Gumbo

Shrimp Bisque

Gumbo Ya Ya

Crawfish Bisque

Gazpacho

Stuffed Potato Soup

Oyster and Artichoke Soup

Lobster and Brie Bisque

Black Bean Soup

Broccoli and Cheese Soup

The Good, the Plaid and the Ugly

Once upon a time "let's do lunch" meant a different thing. To the working man the meal often consisted of what could be stuffed into a metal box and poured into a thermos. This was the common box before concerned parents in Florida brought about its demise in the early 70s.

Purple Parrot Corn and Crab Bisque

½ teaspoon **Clarified Butter (p. 107)**
⅓ cup yellow onion, medium dice
¼ cup green bell peppers, medium dice
¼ cup celery, medium dice
1 teaspoon garlic, minced
1½ teaspoons basil, dried
1 teaspoon white pepper
¼ teaspoon cayenne pepper
½ teaspoon thyme
1½ quarts **Chicken Stock (p. 126)**
¼ cup white wine
1 tablespoon brandy
2 teaspoons Worcestershire
2 teaspoons Crescent City Grill Cayenne and Garlic Sauce
3 cups fresh corn kernels, scraped with pulp (or 2 cans whole kernel corn, drained)
½ cup margarine
½ cup flour
3 cups heavy cream
1 cup Half-n-Half
1 tablespoon Crescent City Grill Creole Seasoning
2 pounds jumbo lump crabmeat, picked of all shell

In an 8-quart saucepan, sweat onion, bell pepper, and celery in clarified butter over medium heat until soft. Add garlic, basil, pepper, cayenne, and thyme. Stir well, making sure that spices are incorporated. Add stock, wine, brandy, Worcestershire, and cayenne and garlic sauce. Cook on high heat 7–10 minutes, then reduce heat to medium. While stock is boiling, make a light peanut butter–colored roux with the margarine and flour. Add the roux to the hot stock and stir thoroughly. Add heavy cream, Half-n-Half, creole seasoning, and crabmeat. Serve hot and garnish with freshly chopped parsley.

Yield: 1 gallon

Crescent City Grill Seafood Gumbo

5 cups **Shrimp Stock (p. 127)**

5 cups **Chicken Stock (p. 126)**

5 gumbo crabs

3½ cups tomatoes, diced with juice

⅔ cup tomato sauce (one 8-ounce can)

2 tablespoons Worcestershire

1 teaspoon black pepper

2 bay leaves

2½ teaspoons basil

1 teaspoon oregano

¾ cup cottonseed oil

1¼ cups flour

2 cups okra, sliced

3 cups yellow onion, medium dice

1½ cups celery, medium dice

1 cup green onion, chopped

1 cup bell peppers, medium dice

½ cup parsley, chopped

3 tablespoons garlic, minced

2 teaspoons cayenne pepper

2 tablespoons Crescent City Grill Creole Seasoning

3 tablespoons Crescent City Grill Cayenne and Garlic Sauce

2 pounds large shrimp, peeled and deveined

1 pound oysters, with juice

1 pound claw crabmeat, picked of all shell

1 pound lump crabmeat, picked of all shell

In a large stockpot, bring first 10 ingredients to a boil. Reduce heat to a brisk simmer and continue to cook, skimming the tomato foam from the top of the stock. While the stock is simmering, make a dark roux using the cottonseed oil and flour. To the roux, add the okra, stirring constantly. Once the okra is incorporated into the roux, add the onion, celery, green onion, bell pepper, parsley, garlic, creole seasoning, and cayenne and garlic sauce, stirring well to incorporate. Cook until the vegetables become soft. Add the shrimp and continue stirring until shrimp turn pink. Add the oysters. Turn up the heat on the simmering stock. Transfer the seafood-roux mixture to the hot stock and stir vigorously until the roux is completely dissolved. Bring the stock to a boil once more and then reduce to a simmer. Add the crabmeat. Remove the gumbo crabs and serve over rice.

Yield: 1 gallon

"There is one thing more exasperating than a wife who can cook and won't and that's a wife who can't cook and will."

—Robert Frost

Shrimp Bisque

2 tablespoons butter
¾ cup green bell peppers, small dice
¼ cup red bell peppers, small dice
1 cup yellow onion, small dice
¼ cup green onion, chopped
2 teaspoons basil, fresh, chopped
2 teaspoons garlic, minced
¼ teaspoon white pepper
1 teaspoon cayenne pepper
2 teaspoons thyme, dried
2 teaspoons Lawry's Seasoned Salt
⅓ cup white wine
2 tablespoons brandy
1 quart **Chicken Stock (p. 126)**
1 quart **Shrimp Stock (p. 127)**
2 tablespoons Worcestershire
1½ teaspoons Crescent City Grill Hot Sauce
1½ cups tomato, fresh, diced
1 pound shrimp, 90–110 count
¾ cup butter
1 cup flour
1 quart whipping cream
1½ cups Half-n-Half
fresh chives and sour cream to garnish

In a 12-quart stockpot, melt 2 tablespoons of butter, then add vegetables and seasonings. Cook until onions become soft and tender. Add wine, brandy, stocks, tomato, Worcestershire, and hot sauce and bring to a simmer. Add shrimp and simmer for 10 minutes. Make a blond roux in a separate skillet with the ¾ cup butter and 1 cup flour. Add the roux to the simmering stock mixture. Add whipping cream and Half-n-Half. Bring soup to a boil and remove from heat. Garnish with fresh chopped chives.

Yield: 1 gallon

Gumbo Ya Ya

2 quarts **Chicken Stock (p. 126)**
1 teaspoon chicken base or bouillon
1 teaspoon shrimp base or bouillon
2 cups tomatoes, fresh, diced, with juice
¼ cup tomato sauce
1 tablespoon Worcestershire
1 teaspoon freshly ground black pepper
1 bay leaf
1 teaspoon basil, dried
1 teaspoon thyme, dried
½ teaspoon oregano, dried
½ cup corn oil
1 cup flour
2 cups yellow onions, medium dice
1½ cups celery, medium dice
¾ cup bell peppers, medium dice
¼ cup green onion, chopped
1 tablespoon garlic, minced
1½ tablespoons Crescent City Grill Creole Sesasoning
2 tablespoons Crescent City Grill Hot Sauce
2 pounds chicken, diced
1 pound andouille
1 tablespoon file powder
2 tablespoons cold water

In a large stockpot, bring the chicken stock and bases to a boil. Add tomatoes, tomato sauce, Worcestershire, and spices. Reduce heat to medium and continue to cook for 20 minutes, skimming the tomato foam from the top of the stock. Make a dark roux using the corn oil and flour. Add onions, celery, bell pepper, garlic, creole seasoning, and hot sauce to roux. Add chicken to roux mixture and cook, stirring constantly. Add andouille and cook 5 minutes more. Add roux mixture to simmering stock, stirring until all is dissolved and incorporated. Separately, mix file powder and cold water together in a blender. Blend on medium speed until you have a gooey paste. Add 1 cup of hot gumbo stock to blender and mix until well blended. Add file mixture to gumbo, stirring well and cook on medium heat for 20 minutes.

Yield: 7 quarts

"Never trust a skinny cook"
Unknown

The Destin Legend

The first restaurant I opened almost closed on opening night. The year was 1987; the restaurant was the Purple Parrot Café.

I didn't know squat about managing a professional kitchen. I was a front-of-the-house guy. My restaurant experience up to that point amounted to working as a waiter for seven years while I was putting myself through college. I became a chef by default.

I hired a talented chef from one of the most popular restaurants in Destin, Florida, to handle the kitchen duties and recipe development. The food he had developed in Destin had been outstanding and would be perfect for our white-tablecloth concept. It was the ideal scenario, he would take care of the back-of-the-house, and I would manage the dining room.

Our new chef was a Destin Legend. His reputation preceded him—not his culinary reputation, mind you, his social reputation. He loved to party, and he was good at it. His escapades and forays into the Destin nightlife and club scene had become legendary.

I wasn't worried. I sobered him up and brought him to Hattiesburg five weeks before we opened. The number one condition of his employment was that he develop all our recipes. Number two was easy: don't drink. He agreed.

As the opening date neared, the legendary chef developed our opening recipes. I trained the waiters. He didn't drink; I didn't either.

We opted for a soft opening. A soft opening, in the restaurant business, means you open the doors without any advertising or promotion. The customers are supposed to trickle in gradually until the staff is accustomed to the volume. This was not to be.

The word was out. We were slammed. Every table in the dining room was seated. We were full as soon as we opened. The line was out the door.

I worked the front-of-the-house as planned, scrambling around greeting customers. I bussed tables and made sure the waiters were giving prompt, professional, and efficient service.

My chef was in the kitchen drinking Heineken.

He had folded under the pressure of a packed house and drank a case of beer out of our cooler. A whole case.

Now You're Cooking

Friday afternoon and the cooks are in rare form in the kitchen of the Purple Parrot. It's easy to imagine the unspoken signals and split-second timing of a team that has trained together for years.

He also drank a bottle of Dr. Tischner's that he had stolen from the Shell station across the street. He was wasted.

I found the Destin Legend lying on the ground behind the restaurant, sweaty, mumbling, and throwing up on the side of the dumpster.

You can lead a chef to water but you can't make him not drink.

The chef was fired on our first night. And, guess who was cooking on the second night? That's right, yours truly, fresh out of college with seven years experience as a waiter and zero as a cook in a commercial kitchen. The first two or three weeks were rocky, but I eventually developed a knack for it.

Although you couldn't have convinced me that night, having to get back in the kitchen to cook turned out to be one of the best things that ever happened to me professionally.

For the next four years I worked sixteen-hour days, six days a week in the Purple Parrot kitchen. I began developing recipes of my own. My recipes began replacing the initial recipes of our beer-binging chef. Corn and Crab Bisque is the exception. It is all that remains of his original menu.

All restaurants have signature dishes. And, thanks to the Destin Legend, Corn and Crab Bisque is one of ours. We would have a small revolt on our hands if we ever tried to take it off the menu. We serve more than a thousand gallons of Corn and Crab Bisque every year.

Clint Taylor, my partner and our sommelier, would normally pair a bold, buttery Chardonnay with Corn and Crab Bisque. I, however, would like to suggest that you curl up with a warm bowl and pop the cap off an ice cold Heineken in remembrance of the opening day chef at the Purple Parrot Café. Just don't drink a whole case.

Crawfish Bisque

3 ounces bacon, rough chopped into ½ inch pieces

½ stick unsalted butter

1 cup yellow onion, medium dice

1 cup celery, medium dice

1 cup bell peppers, medium dice

½ cup carrots, small dice

1 tablespoon garlic, minced

2 teaspoons ground sweet basil

1 teaspoon thyme, dried

2 teaspoons lemon pepper

½ teaspoon Lawry's Seasoned Salt

½ teaspoon white pepper

½ teaspoon celery salt

½ teaspoon cayenne pepper

¼ cup brandy

2 tablespoons white wine

1½ tablespoons Worcestershire

1 teaspoon Crescent City Grill Hot Sauce

½ gallon **Shrimp Stock (p. 127)**

2 cups tomatoes, fresh, chopped (reserve juice and add back to tomatoes)

1 cup **Clarified Butter (p. 107)**, margarine, or oil

1⅓ cups flour

1½ quarts heavy cream

¼ cup parsley, chopped

2 teaspoons paprika

1 tablespoon Crescent City Grill Creole Seasoning

1 tablespoon lemon juice

2 pounds crawfish tail meat, fat drained (do not squeeze crawfish)

Render bacon in a large heavy stockpot over medium high heat. Add butter and melt. Add onion, celery, bell pepper, and carrots and cook until onions are clear and limp. Do not brown. Add garlic and seasonings and stir well. Deglaze with brandy and white wine and stir well. Add Worcestershire, hot sauce, shrimp stock, and tomatoes with juice and bring to a boil. While waiting for stock to boil, make a peanut butter–colored roux using the butter and flour. Add the roux to the stock and stir vigorously. Add heavy cream and return to a low rolling boil. Add remaining ingredients, stir well and remove from heat.

Crawfish do not have to be added until just before serving. If you would like to freeze a portion of this recipe, do not add crawfish. The crawfish can be added after the soup has thawed.

Yield: 1 gallon

"Some people like to paint pictures, or do gardening, or build a boat in the basement. Other people get a tremendous pleasure out of the kitchen, because cooking is just as creative and imaginative an activity as drawing, or wood carving, or music."
—Julia Child

Gazpacho

"Cooking should be a carefully balanced reflection of all the good things of the earth."
—Jean & Pierre Troisgros

4 cups **Tomato Concasse (p. 107)**, large dice
1 cup red bell peppers, small dice
1 cup cucumber, peeled, seeded, small dice
1 cup yellow onion, small dice
1 cup celery, small dice
2 tablespoons garlic, minced
1 cup tomato purée (approximately 2 large tomatoes, peeled and seeded)
½ cup tarragon vinegar
¼ cup extra virgin olive oil
2 cups Beefamato
1 tablespoon salt
1½ teaspoons freshly ground black pepper
parsley, chopped for garnish
Pesto (p. 113)

Place all ingredients in food processor and pulse them for 3–4 minutes. Chill and serve. Garnish with chopped parsley, pesto, or jumbo lump crabmeat.

Yield: 3 quarts

Stuffed Potato Soup

¼ pound bacon, diced large
1½ cups onion, medium dice
1 cup carrots, medium dice
1 cup celery, medium dice
2 teaspoons salt
2 tablespoons garlic, minced
1½ tablespoons black pepper
2 teaspoons Crescent City Grill Creole Seasoning
1 tablespoon Crescent City Grill Cayenne and Garlic Sauce
3 pounds potatoes, peeled, cubed, and cooked to just done
1 quart **Chicken Stock (p. 126)**
2 quarts heavy cream
1½ cups cheddar cheese, shredded
1¼ cups sour cream
½ cup margarine
¾ cup flour
½ cup green onions, chopped fine

Render bacon in a large heavy pot. Add onions, carrots, and celery and cook until onions become clear and soft. Add salt, garlic, pepper, creole seasoning, and hot sauce. Add potatoes and gently stir together (do not mash the potatoes) for a few minutes; add to the soup. Add the chicken stock and bring to a boil. Add heavy cream, cheese, and sour cream and return to a boil. Make a light roux with the margarine and flour and add to the soup. Stir well to incorporate. Remove from heat and add green onions. Garnish with more green onions and chopped bacon.

Yield: 1½ gallons

Oyster and Artichoke Soup

1 stick butter
¼ cup green onion, chopped fine
¼ cup yellow onion, medium dice
¼ cup celery, medium dice
⅓ cup red bell peppers, medium dice
½ teaspoon fresh thyme
2 teaspoons Crescent City Grill Seasoning
1 bay leaf
2 teaspoons garlic, minced
¾ cup flour
3 cups **Chicken Stock (p. 126)**
2½ cups oyster water*
4 cubes chicken bouillon
½ cup oysters, chopped
5 cups heavy cream
1 12-ounce can artichoke hearts, with juice, cut into quarters

In a dutch oven, sauté first 9 ingredients over medium high heat until onions are clear and soft. Add flour slowly, stirring constantly. Do not brown. Cook 2–3 minutes. Dissolve chicken bouillon in oyster water. Add oyster water and chicken stock to vegetable mixture. Add oysters and stir well. Add cream and artichoke hearts.

* If there is not 2½ cups of oyster water, add enough cold tap water to equal 2½ cups.
Yield: 3 quarts

Lobster and Brie Bisque

2 1½-pound lobsters, cooked and cleaned (reserve meat for soup and shells for stock)
1 cup white wine
½ gallon lobster stock*
1 cup tomato paste
2 cups whipping cream
1 bay leaf
1 pound brie, rind removed and cubed
½ teaspoon dried thyme or 2 teaspoons fresh chopped thyme
¼ cup butter
⅓ cup flour
½ cup sour cream
2 3 tablespoons fresh chives, chopped

In a large saucepan, bring the lobster stock, white wine, and tomato paste to a boil. Continue to cook, allowing stock to reduce by half.

Meanwhile, in a double boiler, heat the cream and cheese together until the cheese has melted.

In a medium-size skillet, heat the butter and add flour to make a blond roux. Once stock has reduced, add cream and cheese mixture to the stock. Add roux and bring to a boil. Lower heat and add reserved lobster meat. Place sour cream in a squirt bottle. Ladle soup into serving bowls and decorate the top with thin ribbons of sour cream and freshly chopped chives.

* To make lobster stock, follow the same procedure and recipe for **Shrimp Stock (p. 127)**. It is important to clean the lobster bodies well to remove organs and gills prior to making the stock.
Yield: 3 quarts

"Before you criticize someone, you should walk a mile in their shoes. That way, when you criticize them, you are a mile away from them, and you have their shoes."
—Frieda Norris

Fishy Business

A sign of times past, this neon is in shambles but the message remains the same.

Black Bean Soup

2½ gallons **Chicken Stock (p. 126)**
2 pounds black beans, washed and drained
¾ cup onion, medium dice
¾ cup carrots, medium dice
¾ cup celery, medium dice
½ cup ham, medium dice
3 tablespoons dry mustard
3 tablespoons lemon juice
1 tablespoon garlic powder
½ teaspoon white pepper
½ teaspoon cayenne pepper
⅔ cup red wine
3 tablespoons olive oil or bacon fat

Bring chicken stock to a boil. Add black beans and return to a boil. Lower heat and simmer, stirring occasionally, for 30 minutes. Sauté vegetables in olive oil or bacon fat; add ham and spices. Deglaze with red wine and then add to simmering beans. Add remaining ingredients and simmer 2½–3 hours. Remove 3 cups of the soup and purée in blender or processor; add back into soup. Serve topped with **Tomato Concasse (p. 107)**, rice, and diced onion.
    Yield: 5 quarts

Broccoli and Cheese Soup

¼ cup butter
1½ cups yellow onion, small dice
1 cup celery
1 tablespoon garlic, minced
½ teaspoon white pepper
1 tablespoon black pepper
½ teaspoon cayenne pepper
1 bunch broccoli stalks, chopped in food processor (florettes cut into small pieces)
3 quarts vegetable stock (or water)
1 tablespoon Worcestershire
1 tablespoon Crescent City Grill Cayenne and Garlic Sauce
1 quart cream
1¼ cups butter
1¾ cups flour
2 tablespoons salt
2 cups cheddar cheese, grated

Melt butter in large saucepan over medium heat. Add onion, celery, and garlic and sweat until just tender. Add peppers and vegetable stock and bring to a boil. Add broccoli and cook for 3–5 minutes. Add cream, Worcestershire, salt, and cayenne and garlic sauce. In a separate pan, make a blond roux. Add roux to broccoli stock and bring to a boil. Add grated cheese and stir well.
    Yield: 5 quarts

"The fact is that it takes more than ingredients and technique to cook a good meal. A good cook puts something of himself into the preparation—he cooks with enjoyment, anticipation, spontaneity, and he is willing to experiment."—Pearl Bailey

Seafood Entrees

Cioppino

Baked Shrimp and Squash

Jumbo Lump Crab Cakes

Seafood Lasagna

BBQ Shrimp

Shrimp Creole

Crawfish Etouffee

Shrimp and Grits with Chanterelle
Mushrooms

Paneed Redfish with Creole Cream

Catfish 589

Lobster Risotto

Softshell Crabs
with Honey-Roasted Nuts
and Three Light Sauces

Eggplant Dauphine

Crab Cakes Monica

Redfish Pontchartrain

Grouper Orleans

Snapper Madeira

Bayou Redfish

Horseradish-Crusted Salmon
with Spinach Gratin

Grouper Tchoupitoulas

Seafood Napoleon

Grilled Tuna with Orange Ginger
Butter Sauce

Eggplant Bayou Teche

Networking

Behind this shrimp boat
in Ocean Springs is the
Anderson compound. These
ships work long hours in
extreme weather in search
of the pink delicacy.

Cioppino

Cioppino Stock

¼ cup olive oil
¼ cup butter
1½ cups onions, medium dice
1½ cups leeks, hand-chopped fine, white part only
1½ cups green bell peppers, medium dice
1⅓ cups carrots, small dice
1 cup celery, medium dice
¼ cup fresh fennel, chopped fine
4 28-ounce cans crushed tomatoes, highest quality, strained, roughly chopped (reserve liquid)
1 6-ounce can tomato paste
2½ quarts water (or stock)
2 tablespoons salt
1½ tablespoons Tabasco
1 tablespoon oregano, dried
1 tablespoon basil, dried
1 tablespoon thyme, dried
3 bay leaves
1 tablespoon Crescent City Grill Creole Seasoning

Sauté onions in olive oil and butter. Do not brown. Add leeks, green pepper, carrots, celery, and fennel and cook 5–10 minutes until soft. Add remaining ingredients and bring to a boil. When stock begins boiling, immediately reduce heat. Cover and simmer 2 hours stirring frequently. This stock should be made a day ahead of time and refrigerated.

Yield: 1¼ gallons

Cioppino

½ cup olive oil
2 pounds shrimp, 31–35 count, peeled and deveined
1 pound sea scallops
1 pound redfish pieces (about the size of the scallops)
1 pound fresh mussels, cleaned and beards removed
1 pound jumbo lump crabmeat
1 cup **Seasoned Flour (p. 107)**
2 tablespoons garlic, minced
1 cup white wine
1½ quarts cioppino stock
toasted French bread
fresh chopped parsley for garnish

Lightly dust shrimp, scallops, and redfish in seasoned flour. In a very large skillet, heat olive oil over high heat and sauté the seafood that has been dusted with flour. Cook the seafood for 3–5 minutes, then add the garlic. Cook for 1–2 more minutes, deglaze with wine, and add the cioppino stock. Add mussels. Cover and simmer for 6–7 minutes. When the mussels open, add crabmeat and cook for 1–2 more minutes. Divide seafood into serving dishes and garnish with parsley. Serve with toasted French bread.

Yield: 6–10 servings

Baked Shrimp and Squash

6 cups squash, sliced into ½-inch discs
½ cup **Clarified Butter (p. 107)**
2 tablespoons garlic, minced
1 teaspoon salt
1 teaspoon freshly ground pepper
1 tablespoon Crescent City Grill Creole Seasoning
green onions, ½ cup chopped and ¼ cup sliced
3 cups fresh, large shrimp (36–42 count), peeled and deveined
1 tablespoon Old Bay Seasoning
½ cup onion, medium dice
¼ cup red bell peppers, medium dice
¼ cup green bell peppers, medium dice
4 tablespoons butter
¾ cup Parmesan cheese, freshly grated
1 cup cheddar cheese, grated
1 cup sour cream
1 tablespoon Crescent City Grill Cayenne and Garlic Sauce
1 cup Ritz Cracker crumbs, pulsed until fine in processor
2 tablespoons parsley, chopped

Sauté the squash, ¼ cup clarified butter, 1 tablespoon garlic, salt, pepper, creole seasoning, and chopped green onion until the squash is al dente. Pour into a stainless steel mixing bowl. Sauté shrimp, ¼ cup clarified butter, Old Bay Seasoning, 1 tablespoon garlic, onion, red bell pepper, and green bell pepper until the shrimp are pink and cooked through. Transfer the shrimp to the mixing bowl with the squash. To the bowl, add 4 tablespoons butter, ½ cup Parmesan, cheddar, sour cream, sliced green onion, and cayenne and garlic sauce.

Separately, mix together the Ritz crumbs, ¼ cup Parmesan and parsley.

Place equal portions of the shrimp and squash mixture into a 3-quart casserole dish and top with the cracker crumb mixture. Bake at 350° until bubbly.

Yield: 8–10 servings

Jumbo Lump Crab Cakes

¼ pound butter
½ cup flour
1 cup green onions, small dice
2 teaspoons salt
½ teaspoon cayenne pepper
½ teaspoon black pepper
2 cups milk
2 eggs, beaten
1 pound jumbo lump crabmeat, picked of all shell
40 saltine crackers (2 sleeves), finely crushed in food processor
1 cup breadcrumbs
2 tablespoons Crescent City Grill Creole Seasoning

Make a light blond roux using the flour and butter. Add the green onions, salt, and cayenne and cook for 2–3 minutes. Slowly add the milk and stir constantly until the mixture thickens (approximately 4 minutes). Remove from heat.

In a mixing bowl, combine the egg with the crabmeat and the cracker crumbs. Mix gently so as not to break up the lumps of crabmeat. Gently fold in the milk mixture and let cool. Divide the mixture into 3-ounce patties.

In a shallow bowl, combine the breadcrumbs and the creole seasoning. Dredge the crab patties in the breadcrumb mixture and sauté over medium high heat in a small amount of cottonseed oil until lightly browned on each side. Finish cooking crab cakes in a 400° oven for 5–6 minutes. Serve with **Seafood Remoulade (p. 118)**.

Yield: 15 cakes

"Never work before breakfast; if you have to work before breakfast, eat your breakfast first."—Josh Billings

The Great Cioppino Incident

When I am asked to be a guest lecturer at the University of Southern Mississippi's restaurant management classes, I usually talk to the students about the numerous business mistakes I've made over the years. I do so with the hope that once the students open their own businesses they won't make the same mistakes. One of my favorite lecture topics is "The Great Cioppino Incident."

The Great Cioppino Incident occurred during the early months of my first restaurant's opening. Cioppino (Chuh-PEE-noh) is a hearty, tomato-based seafood stew, which was brought to San Francisco by Italian immigrants around the turn of the twentieth century. Its origins can be traced to the classic seafood stew from Provence—bouillabaisse (BOOL-yuh-BAYZ).

Cioppino contains tomatoes, fish, shellfish, olive oil, and white wine. And, in its typical form, so does bouillabaisse. But bouillabaisse also contains saffron and is typically served over slices of French bread. Bouillabaisse also has enough garlic in it to keep you as lonely as an orthodontist in London.

Let me clarify that I don't speak a syllable of French. I can speak bogus-menu-French, but early in my restaurant career, I couldn't even do that. Nor am I a classically trained chef. I began my restaurant career as a waiter and was thrown into the kitchen on our second night due to the firing of our chef on opening night.

I also opened my first restaurant with limited dining-out experience. The first time I offered cioppino as a feature in the Purple Parrot, I had never eaten it in a restaurant, I had never heard anyone talk about it, and therefore, I had no idea how to pronounce it. I developed the dish, nonetheless, and it tasted great.

Being excited about this new offering I shifted into high-powered-sales mode and greeted customers at the door with the bravado of an all-knowing restaurant veteran telling them, "Make sure and try our cioppino" (which I pronounced SEE-OP-i-NOE). I continued my pitch with, "It's great, and it tastes a lot like bouillabaisse" (which I pronounced BOE-luh-BASSIE). Throughout the restaurant all of our waiters were using

47

the same incorrect pronunciations when they gave their oral presentations to customers at the table. They were taking cues from their esteemed and knowledgeable leader, me.

After a few weeks, one of our regular customers had pity on me. She pulled me aside and discreetly corrected my pronunciation of the classic restaurant dishes, but only after I had mispronounced both dishes hundreds of times to scores of customers and employees.

The Great Cioppino Incident used to keep me up at night. Since those days, I have fought off the strong urge to seek out those early customers and tell them, "I know how to pronounce bouillabaisse and cioppino now. I really, really do, I promise. Please come back to the restaurant, sit down, and let me pronounce them for you!"

The lesson I learned that day was: If you don't know it, don't fake it. And that is what I always tell the students.

So, if a friend ever offers you a warm bowl of SEE-OP-i-NOE, please send him or her back to the Purple Parrot so I can redeem myself, clear my conscience, and show that I now know how to speak bogus-menu-French.

Seafood Lasagna

1 package lasagna sheets

2 pounds ricotta cheese

5 eggs

½ cup Romano cheese, grated

1 teaspoon white pepper

1 teaspoon salt

1 tablespoon garlic, granulated

1 pound backfin or jumbo lump crabmeat, picked clean of all shells

½ cup butter

1 pound small shrimp, 90–110 count

2 tablespoons Crescent City Grill Creole Seasoning

1 pound frozen spinach, thawed and squeezed dry

¼ cup Parmesan cheese

black pepper, ground fresh, to taste

To prepare before assembling lasagna:

Cook lasagna sheets, rinse them under cool water, and lay them out flat. Lightly oil the pasta sheets so that they do not stick together. Combine ricotta cheese, eggs, Romano, white pepper, granulated garlic, and salt. Set aside. In a large skillet, heat the butter. Season shrimp with creole seasoning and sauté until pink. Remove from heat and set aside. Mix the spinach with Parmesan cheese and black pepper. Set aside.

Béchamel Sauce

1 cup butter

1 cup flour

½ cup whole milk, hot

2 tablespoons Worcestershire

2 teaspoons Crescent City Grill Hot Sauce

1 tablespoon salt

2 teaspoons black pepper, ground fresh

1½ cups mozzarella cheese, shredded

½ cup fresh parsley, chopped

In a sauce pot, melt butter and add flour to make roux. Add the hot milk to roux and stir until smooth. Add Worcestershire, Tabasco, salt, and pepper. Divide the sauce in half and set other half aside for later use.

To assemble lasagna:

Preheat oven to 300°. Coat the bottom of a 9x14-inch casserole dish with a light layer of the béchamel. Alternate layers of pasta sheets with béchamel, crabmeat, ricotta mixture, shrimp, and spinach mixture. Reserve enough ricotta mixture for the top layer. (Remember, half of the béchamel is for later). Top it off with the shredded mozzarella. Cover the lasagna tightly with a layer of waxed paper and then a layer of heavy duty foil. Place in the preheated oven and bake for 1 hour and 20 minutes. Turn the oven up to 450°, remove foil and wax paper. Brown the top of the lasagna. Remove from oven and let set at least 15 minutes before cutting. Cut desired portions of lasagna and place on a serving dish. Ladle 2–3 ounces of reserved béchamel sauce (warmed) over lasagna. Garnish with fresh parsley.

Yield: 8–12 servings

"The smell of good bread baking, like the sound of lightly flowing water, is indescribable in its evocation of innocence and delight."—M. F. K. Fisher

BBQ Shrimp

"Eat butter first, and eat it last, and live till a hundred years be past."—Old Dutch proverb

BBQ Shrimp Stock

2 cups white wine
1 quart **Shrimp Stock (p.127)**
¾ cup Crescent City Grill Creole Seasoning
½ cup Worcestershire sauce
½ cup lemon juice
3 tablespoons paprika
2 tablespoons garlic, minced
2 tablespoons liquid crab boil
¾ cup creole mustard
4 bay leaves
1 tablespoon Crescent City Grill Hot Sauce

Bring all ingredients to a boil, immediately remove from heat and cool (can be made 2–3 days ahead of time). Make sure to stir the cold BBQ shrimp stock vigorously before adding it to the skillet.

Yield: 2 quarts stock

BBQ Shrimp

6 ounces **Clarified Butter (p. 107)**
2 pounds shrimp, unpeeled, head-on
2 tablespoons garlic, minced
2 tablespoons cracked black peppercorns
2 cups BBQ Shrimp Stock

Melt clarified butter in a skillet and add unpeeled shrimp (head-on). Sauté until shrimp begins to turn pink. Add cracked black peppercorns and garlic. Add BBQ shrimp stock and cook until shrimp are just done. Serve with plenty of toasted French bread for dipping.

Shrimp Creole

2 pounds shrimp, 31–35 count, peeled and deveined
1 tablespoon Old Bay Seasoning
¼ cup **Clarified Butter (p. 107)**
1 tablespoon garlic, minced
½ cup white wine
1 cup green onions, chopped
1 tablespoon Crescent City Grill Creole Seasoning
1 quart **Crescent City Grill Creole Sauce (p. 110)**, hot
8 cups white rice, cooked and seasoned
fresh parsley, chopped
toasted French bread

In a very large skillet, heat butter over a high heat. Season shrimp with Old Bay Seasoning. Place seasoned shrimp in the hot butter. Cook 3 minutes. Add garlic and sauté for 2 minutes. Add green onions and creole seasoning and deglaze with white wine. Let wine reduce by half. Add creole sauce and bring to a heavy simmer. Remove from heat and serve over rice. Garnish with parsley and serve with toasted French bread.

Yield: 6–8 servings

Crawfish Etouffeé

2 tablespoons **Clarified Butter (p. 107)**
2 pounds crawfish tail meat, lightly drained
3 tablespoons garlic, minced
1½ cups green onion, sliced
3 ounces white wine
1½ quarts **Etouffeé Stock (p. 118)**
8 cups cooked white rice

Heat clarified butter. Sauté garlic quickly but do not brown. Add crawfish and cook for 2 minutes until hot. Add green onion and deglaze with white wine. Add etouffee stock and heat thoroughly. Divide rice evenly into serving dishes; spoon etouffee over rice. Garnish with lemon and fresh parsley, and serve with buttered and toasted French bread.

Yield: 10–12 servings

Shrimp and Grits with Chanterelle Mushrooms

3 ounces **Clarified Butter (p. 107)**
2 pounds shrimp, 31-35 count, peeled and deveined
2 tablespoons Old Bay Seasoning
1 tablespoon garlic, crushed
½ pound chanterelle mushrooms, cleaned well and thinly sliced
3 ounces brandy
1 cup **Caramelized Onions (p. 101)**
1 tablespoon Crescent City Grill Cayenne and Garlic Sauce
6 ounces **Beurre Blanc (p. 112)**
1 recipe **Andouille Cheese Grits (p. 95)**

Season shrimp with Old Bay Seasoning. Heat butter over medium high heat. Add shrimp. Cook 1–2 minutes, stirring well. Add garlic and cook for another minute. Add mushrooms and caramelized onions and continue cooking until mushrooms are tender. Deglaze with brandy and let liquid reduce slightly. Remove from heat and add beurre blanc. Divide grits onto serving dishes. Divide shrimp and mushroom topping over the grits and garnish with chopped parsley.

Yield: 6 servings

"After a good dinner, one can forgive anybody, even one's relatives."—Oscar Wilde

Dinner Conversation

When my wife and I have guests over for dinner, a frequent topic of conversation is, "If you could invite six people in all history to dinner who would they be?" My list is ever changing, based on my heroes. If I made the list today it would include Louis Armstrong, Willie Morris, Muddy Waters, Paul McCartney, Shelby Foote, and Winston Churchill. Heroes all.

Willie Morris, a fellow Mississippian, was a great writer with a highly developed intellect. I never met him, and I am a poorer man for it. Louis Armstrong, a New Orleanian, invented jazz, and toured the world while playing it for decades. Muddy Waters, another fellow Mississippian, invented the electric blues, which later morphed into rock and roll. Paul McCartney perfected the rock and roll that Muddy Waters invented. Shelby Foote, a Delta Mississippian, was friends with Mr. Faulkner and can tell you more about the Civil War than Grant and Lee combined.

Winston Churchill, one of my all-time heroes, would be the ultimate dinner guest. Churchill had one of the most brilliant minds of the twentieth century. In addition to his political and military accomplishments, he is responsible for the greatest comeback line of all time, which, by the way, was delivered at a dinner table. He was seated beside Lady Astor, who complained, "If you were my husband, I'd put poison in your coffee." To which Churchill replied, "If you were my wife, I'd drink it."

Churchill's second greatest comeback was given to Bessie Braddock, a member of Parliament, who complained about Churchill being drunk. To which Churchill replied, "And you, madam, are ugly. But I shall be sober in the morning."

Foote and Churchill could discuss military strategy while Waters and McCartney talk music. Morris and Armstrong would talk of their experiences being expatriated southerners and artists who returned home at the top of their craft. I would ask a thousand and one questions and never once complain of Churchill's drunkenness.

Some might find fault in the fact that there aren't any women at my table. But my wife Jill would be there. She is my number-one hero.

What a dinner we would have, two knighted Brits and four southerners (six if you count my wife and me) eating plenty of fresh vegetables from the Hattiesburg Farmers' Market and my grandmother's leg of lamb. The dinner table conversation would stand

Room at the Table

Learning which forks go where and how to polish silverware are essential to the proper upbringing of a southern child. The formality and the ritual of dining together suggests a spirituality that when we eat, we share more than food.

as the crown jewel in the archives of the Oral History Department at the University of Southern Mississippi.

Some of the most engaging conversations I have been a part of have taken place around the dinner table. As a child, I knew families who never talked during meals. Someone said the blessing and the next words you heard were "May I be excused?" I am grateful that I didn't grow up in a house like that. We talked at the dinner table at my house. As a matter of fact, we never stopped talking, and we talked loudly. It was hard to get a word in at the St. John house. It is still that way. Conversation at the family dinner table is important, as long as you aren't talking while your mouth is full.

Taking time to dine with family has become the exception rather than the rule. As a society, it is our loss.

Paneed Redfish with Creole Cream

4 7-ounce portions redfish filet
3 tablespoons Crescent City Grill Creole Seasoning
1 cup flour
½ cup **Clarified Butter** (p. 107)
1½ cups **Creole Cream Sauce** (p. 113)

Preheat oven to 450°. Mix 3 tablespoons creole seasoning with 1 cup flour. In a heavy sauté pan over medium high heat, add enough clarified butter to eventually come up halfway on the sides of the fish filets. Sprinkle creole seasoning on both sides of fish filets. Dust the filets in the seasoned flour, shaking off all excess flour. Panee filets in clarified butter for approximately 2 minutes on each side. Transfer fish to a sheet pan and finish cooking in the oven. Do not overcook the fish. In the skillet, drain all excess butter and heat creole cream sauce over medium heat. Place fish filets on 4 separate plates and top with equal amounts of the sauce.

Shrimp, crawfish, crabmeat, green onions, chives, garlic, and andouille sausage, in any combination, can be added to this sauce.

Yield: 4 servings

Catfish 589

4 8-ounce catfish filets
catfish breading
¼ cup **Clarified Butter** (p. 107)
2 cups mushrooms, cleaned and sliced
½ cup green onions, sliced
1 pound crawfish tail meat
1 cup **Creole Cream Sauce** (p. 113)
cottonseed oil for frying fish

Preheat oven to 400°. In a cast-iron skillet, bread and fry 4 8-ounce catfish filets in cottonseed oil. Set them aside and keep them warm. Sauté mushrooms in margarine over medium high heat until they become soft. Add green onions and crawfish and continue to sauté for 1–2 minutes. Add creole cream sauce and cook approximately 3 minutes until thickened. Place 4 fried catfish filets in 4 single-serving oven-proof dishes or small cast-iron skillets. Pour creole cream sauce over the top and bake in oven for 5–7 minutes.

Yield: 4 servings

"There is no sight on earth more appealing than the sight of a woman making dinner for someone she loves."
—Thomas Wolfe

Lobster Risotto

Softshell Crabs with Honey-Roasted Nuts and Three Light Sauces

"Indigestion is charged by God with enforcing morality on the stomach."—Victor Hugo

3 1½-pound lobsters, cooked and cleaned (reserve meat for risotto and use shells and bodies for stock)
3 tablespoons **Clarified Butter (p. 107)**
½ pound aborio rice
½ cup shallots, chopped fine
1 quart hot lobster stock*
1 bay leaf
1 bunch asparagus, cut into 2-inch pieces
¾ cup whipping cream
½ cup Parmesan cheese, grated
2 teaspoons salt
1 teaspoon freshly ground black pepper
¼ cup fresh parsley, chopped
1 tablespoon fresh thyme, chopped

In a large skillet, heat butter over low medium heat. Add shallots and cook until they become soft. Add rice and stir continually until rice gets hot. Do not brown. Reduce heat to low and add one cup of stock. Turn heat down so that the stock is just barely simmering. Continue to stir constantly. As the stock is absorbed, add more stock in small amounts. Continue this process until the grains have become slightly tender.

Just before adding last ladle of stock, add asparagus pieces and lobster meat. Add remaining stock. Add cream, Parmesan, salt, pepper, and herbs and cook until thickened, about 4–5 minutes. Serve immediately.

* To make lobster stock, follow the same procedure and recipe for **Shrimp Stock (p. 127)**. It is important to clean the lobster bodies well to remove organs and gills prior to making the stock.

Yield: 6 servings

6 softshell crabs, cleaned
2 cups milk
2 eggs
1 tablespoon tarragon, dried
4 tablespoons Crescent City Grill Cayenne and Garlic Sauce
2 tablespoons Crescent City Grill Creole Seasoning
peanut oil, for frying crabs
3 cups **Seasoned Flour (p. 107)**
½ cup **Choron Sauce (p. 111)**
1 cup **Beurre Blanc (p. 112)**
1 cup **Lemon Meuniere (p. 122)**
½ cup **Honey-Roasted Nuts (p. 101)**

Combine milk, eggs, tarragon, cayenne and garlic sauce, and creole seasoning. Mix well. Gently drop the crabs in the seasoned milk mixture and place all in the refrigerator and marinate for at least 6 hours. When you are ready to cook the crabs, heat peanut oil to 350° in a heavy skillet. Take crabs out of the milk mixture one at a time and lightly dust them in the seasoned flour. Be careful to keep all of the legs attached and gently separate the legs that stick together. Slowly glide the crab (shell side down) into the hot oil, being careful not to splash. Cook approximately 2 minutes and turn over for another minute. Remove the crabs and drain on paper towels. Place 1 tablespoon choron sauce in the center of plates and top with a softshell crab. Ladle 2 ounces each of beurre blanc and lemon meuniere sauce over crab. Sprinkle honey-roasted nuts over crab and garnish with chopped parsley and lemon.

Yield: 6 servings

Eggplant Dauphine

18 eggplant rounds
1 cup **Seasoned Flour** (p. 107)
1½ cups **Eggwash** (p. 107)
1½ cups seasoned breadcrumbs
cottonseed oil, for deep-frying
½ cup **Clarified Butter** (p. 107)
2 pounds shrimp, 31–36 count, peeled and deveined
2 teaspoons Old Bay Seasoning
1 pound crawfish tail meat
3 tablespoons garlic, minced
1½ cups sliced mushrooms
½ cup white wine
½ cup green onion, chopped
1 cup **Creole Cream Sauce** (p. 113)
1 cup **Parmesan Cream Sauce** (p. 117)
1 cup Romano cheese
fresh parsley for garnish

Peel eggplant and cut into round slices ¼ inch thick and 3 inches in diameter. Marinate eggplant in salted ice water.

To prepare eggplant wheels, dust the wheels with seasoned flour, shake off excess flour, dip them in the eggwash, and coat with breadcrumbs. Fry, a few at a time. Be careful not to overload the oil. Drain on paper towels. Hold in a warm oven while you prepare seafood mixture.

In a large skillet, heat butter over medium high heat. Season the shrimp with Old Bay Seasoning and sauté 3–4 minutes. Add mushrooms, garlic, and crawfish meat, and continue to cook for another 4–5 minutes. Deglaze with white wine and reduce by half. Add creole cream sauce and Parmesan cream sauce and bring to a simmer. Stir in ¾ cup of the Romano cheese and green onion. On serving plates, layer the eggplant wheels with seafood mixture and garnish with parsley and remaining Romano cheese.

Yield: 6 servings

Crab Cakes Monica

12 **Jumbo Lump Crab Cakes** (p. 45)
4 tablespoons **Clarified Butter** (p. 107)
1½ cups green onions, sliced
½ pound shrimp, peeled and deveined
2 tablespoons Old Bay Seasoning
2 tablespoons garlic, minced
6 ounces **Parmesan Cream Sauce** (p. 117)
10 ounces **Creole Cream Sauce** (p. 113)

Preheat oven to 375°. Heat the clarified butter in a large skillet over medium heat. Brown both sides of the crab cakes. Remove from heat. Place crab cakes on a baking sheet and bake them in the oven for 8–10 minutes. While crab cakes are baking, return skillet to heat. Drain excess butter leaving 2 tablespoons. Season shrimp with Old Bay Seasoning and sauté for 1–2 minutes until shrimp start to turn pink. Add garlic and green onion and continue cooking for several minutes. Add Parmesan cream sauce and creole cream sauce. Bring to a simmer and cook for 2–3 minutes. Remove crab cakes from oven and place on serving dishes. Divide topping evenly over crab cakes.

Yield: 6 servings

"In cooking, as in all the arts, simplicity is the sign of perfection."—Curnonsky

Sunday Buffet Dash

When I was a child, my family ate three Sunday lunches a month at my grandmother's house. On the fourth Sunday we ate at the Hattiesburg Country Club. The most memorable part of eating Sunday lunch at the Country Club was not the food, but the drive there.

Just outside the city limits in a pristine setting of tall pines and flowering azaleas, the Country Club was the perfect destination for Sunday lunch. The only thing that marred the perfection of the occasion was the church traffic on the way. Sunday lunch at the Country Club was always a race to beat the Baptists to the buffet.

As soon as the organist hit the last note of the final hymn at Main Street United Methodist Church, my mother would scoop my brother and me up and say "Let's get a move on boys, we've got to get to the Club before the Baptists let out."

I could detect movement out of the corner of my eye, as our choir was midway through the doxology. I didn't dare turn around, but I knew what it was: three or four other families were inching their way toward the door, trying to sneak out of church early to beat the Baptists. Moments later, the church doors would fly open and hundreds of hungry Methodists would rush down the steps and race out to Main Street as if there was a fire in the sanctuary.

Gentlemen, start your engines. The race was on!

In those days, Main Street United Methodist Church was flanked on three sides by Hattiesburg's largest Baptist churches; First Baptist to the south, Temple Baptist to the west, and Main Street Baptist to the north. It took great planning to plot the route to the Club that would offer the least resistance.

I used to picture my mother as the female version of General George S. Patton, pulling a top-secret map from her purse, spreading it on top of the old yellow Plymouth while she calculated the best route.

I can see her now, my mom, in the church parking lot, using methods of post-worship strategy and tactical precision not seen since Patton planned his invasion of France. "We'll get through the Baptists' west flank boys, but we're going to have to do the Super-Secret-7th-Street-Cut-Off-Maneuver!"

The race intensified!

The Baptists might have had strength in numbers, but we Methodists could be very determined and quite clever when it came to eating.

At my church, we even began our morning service five minutes earlier than other churches. We still do, 10:55 a.m., sharp. I assumed we started early because, as Methodists, we just couldn't wait to begin our worship service. I came to believe later that it might have been the idea of one of the elders in our church, who had missed that last piece of white meat on the buffet one too many times. "Let's move that start time up five minutes preacher, I am withering away to nothing but skin and bones."

I had Baptist friends who began to get antsy if the preacher's traditional post-sermon invitation went on too long. A good Sunday for the Baptist preacher, with a lot of converts coming down to the altar to be saved, also meant getting out late and being at the back of the buffet line with the last pick of the desserts.

As a kid, I heard a rumor that there was a Baptist gentleman who, after singing the 37th consecutive chorus of "Just As I Am," made a mad dash out of the sanctuary with his kids in tow, yelling half-crazed at the top of his lungs, "Those Methodists are going to eat all the roast beef!" He and his family are Episcopalians now.

Nowadays, two of Hattiesburg's biggest Baptist churches have moved out west with the gated communities and shopping centers. Unfortunately, there is no longer a traffic problem in downtown Hattiesburg on Sundays. But, for old times sake, I would like to get my mom behind the wheel just one more time and have her weave in and out of that Baptist traffic on our wild Sunday Buffet Dash.

Ah yes, Methodists on their way to the lunch, just like Patton on his way to the Seine.

Redfish Pontchartrain

6 redfish filets, 6-8 ounces each
4 tablespoons **Clarified Butter (p. 107)**
1 cup **Seasoned Flour (p. 107)**
4 cups sliced button mushrooms
1½ cups green onions, sliced
12 ounces jumbo lump crabmeat
3 ounces white wine
1 tablespoon garlic, minced
1½ cups **Lemon Meuniere (p. 122)**

Preheat oven to 350°. Put seasoned flour into a large shallow pan. Lightly flour filets. Heat butter in a large skillet over medium high heat and brown both sides of fish. Do not overload the sauté pan. After fish is brown, place filets on baking sheet and cook in oven for 5–10 minutes, depending upon the thickness of the filet. Place mushrooms in skillet and sauté until tender. Add garlic, crab, and green onions and cook 2–3 more minutes. Deglaze with white wine and let wine reduce by one-half. Remove from heat and add the lemon meuniere. Remove filets from oven and place in serving dishes. Evenly divide topping over fish and serve. Garnish with lemon and fresh parsley.

   Yield: 6–8 servings

Grouper Orleans

6 grouper filets, 6–8 ounces each
¼ cup **Clarified Butter (p. 107)**
1 cup **Seasoned Flour (p. 107)**
½ pound shrimp, peeled and deveined
2 tablespoons garlic, minced
4 cups mushrooms, sliced
1½ cups green onions, sliced
3 ounces white wine
1¼ cups **Creole Cream Sauce (p. 113)**
½ cup Romano cheese
¼ cup **Parmesan Cream Sauce (p. 117)**
¼ cup parsley, chopped
¼ cup Romano cheese, grated

Preheat oven to 350°. Place seasoned flour into large shallow pan. Lightly flour filets. Heat butter in a large skillet over medium high heat and lightly brown both sides of fish. Do not overload the sauté pan. After fish is brown, place filets on baking sheet and cook in oven for 5–10 minutes, depending upon the thickness of the filet. Sauté shrimp for 2–3 minutes until they begin to turn pink. Add mushrooms and cook until tender. Add garlic and green onions and cook an additional 2–3 minutes. Add creole cream sauce and Parmesan cream sauce and bring to a simmer. Remove from heat; stir in cheese. Divide evenly and spoon over fish. Garnish with fresh parsley and grated Romano.

   Yield: 6 servings

"A man's palate can, in time, become accustomed to anything."—Napoleon Bonaparte

Snapper Madeira

"Omit and substitute! That's how recipes should be written. Please don't ever get so hung up on published recipes that you forget that you can omit and substitute."—Jeff Smith

6 snapper filets, 6–8 ounces each
1 cup **Seasoned Flour (p. 107)**
4 tablespoons **Clarified Butter (p. 107)**
4 cups mushrooms, sliced
1 12–ounce can artichoke hearts, drained
3 tablespoons garlic, minced
4 ounces Madeira wine
1 cup **Lemon Meuniere (p. 122)**
1½ cups green onions, sliced

Preheat oven to 350°. Place seasoned flour into large shallow pan. Lightly flour filets. Heat butter in a large skillet over medium high heat and brown both sides of fish. After fish is brown, place filets on baking sheet and cook in oven for 5–10 minutes, depending upon the thickness of the filet. While fish is baking, sauté mushrooms in clarified butter until tender. Add artichoke hearts, green onions, and garlic and continue to cook for 3–4 minutes. Deglaze with Madeira wine and reduce wine by one-half. Remove from heat and add lemon meuniere sauce. Top fish and garnish with lemon and fresh parsley.

Yield: 6 servings

Bayou Redfish

1 cup **Seasoned Flour (p. 107)**
6 redfish filets, 6–8 ounces each
4 tablespoons butter
¼ cup red bell peppers, small dice
¼ cup green bell peppers, small dice
¼ cup red onion, small dice
1½ cups diced tomatoes
1 tablespoon garlic, minced
24 shrimp, large, peeled and deveined
8 ounces crawfish tail meat
1 tablespoon Crescent City Grill Creole Seasoning
1½ cups heavy cream
4 ounces **Parmesan Cream Sauce (p. 117)**

Preheat oven to 350°. Place seasoned flour into large shallow pan. Lightly flour filets. Heat butter in a large skillet over medium high heat and brown both sides of fish. Do not overload the sauté pan. After fish is brown, place filets on baking sheet and cook in oven for 5–10 minutes. In a skillet, sauté shrimp for 2–3 minutes, add crawfish, garlic, bell peppers, and onion. Cook for 3–4 more minutes. Add tomato, creole seasoning, cream, and Parmesan cream sauce and bring to a simmer. Cook 3–4 more minutes and remove from heat. Place fish on serving plates and divide topping evenly over filets.

Yield: 6 servings

Horseradish-Crusted Salmon with Spinach Gratin

4–6 ounces **Clarified Butter (p. 107)**
6 6-ounce salmon filets
1 cup **Seasoned Flour (p. 107)**
1 cup **Eggwash (p.107)**
1 cup prepared horseradish
2 cups breadcrumbs, coarse
2 leeks, white part only, cut into a very fine julienne
½ cup cornstarch
cottonseed oil, for deep-frying leeks
1 recipe of **Spinach Gratin (p. 99)**
1½ cups **Red Pepper Coulis (p. 105)**

Preheat oven to 375°. To bread the salmon, place filets in seasoned flour and dust lightly. Dip filets into eggwash. Press the filets, skin side down into breadcrumbs, spread the top half of the filet with horseradish and then coat the horseradish with breadcrumbs.

In a large skillet, heat butter over a medium heat. Place salmon, horseradish side down, and cook until golden brown. Turn filets over. Brown the bottom side, then remove filets and place on a baking sheet. Cook salmon in the oven for 12–14 minutes.

To make the frizzled leeks, preheat to 350° enough oil for deep-frying. Lightly dust the finely julienned leeks with the cornstarch. Drop them into hot oil. Gently stir them and remove when golden brown. Drain on a paper towel. This may be done 1–2 hours in advance.

To serve, fill in the center of a serving plate with the spinach gratin. Place the salmon in the center of the plate and top with frizzled leeks.

Yield: 6 servings

Grouper Tchoupitoulas

6 grouper filets, 6–8 ounces each
1 cup **Seasoned Flour (p. 107)**
4 tablespoons **Clarified Butter (p. 107)**
12 ounces crawfish tail meat
3 tablespoons garlic
3 ounces white wine
1 cup Crescent City Grill Creole Seasoning
¾ cup **Beurre Blanc (p. 112)**
1½ cups green onion, sliced

Preheat oven to 350°. Place seasoned flour into large shallow pan. Lightly flour filets. Heat butter in a large skillet over medium high heat and lightly brown both sides of fish. Do not overload the sauté pan. After fish is brown, place filets on baking sheet and cook in oven for 5–10 minutes. In the skillet, sauté crawfish and garlic over medium high heat for 2–3 minutes. Add green onion and deglaze with white wine. Reduce wine by one-half. Add creole seasoning. Remove from heat and add beurre blanc. Place filets on serving dishes and evenly divide topping over fish.

Yield: 6 servings

"The potato, like man, was not meant to dwell alone."
—Shila Hibben

Seafood Napoleon

"I believe that if ever I had to practice cannibalism, I might manage if there were enough tarragon around."
—James Beard

18 eggplant slices, peeled and sliced into ¼-inch rounds, 3 inches in diameter

1 cup **Seasoned Flour** (p. 107)

2 cups **Eggwash** (p. 107)

1½ cups seasoned breadcrumbs

cottonseed oil, for deep-frying

3 tablespoons **Clarified Butter** (p. 107)

1½ pounds shrimp, large (24 count)

¾ pound red snapper, cut into 1½ inch pieces

1 tablespoon Crescent City Grill Creole Seasoning

½ pound crawfish tail meat

½ pound jumbo lump crabmeat

1 tablespoon garlic, minced

1 cup green onion, sliced

1 cup white wine

1 teaspoon saffron

1½ cups **Beurre Blanc** (p. 112)

To prepare eggplant wheels, dust the wheels with seasoned flour, dip them in eggwash, and coat with breadcrumbs. Fry wheels a few at a time, being careful not to overload the oil. Drain on paper towels. Hold in a warm oven while you prepare seafood mixture.

In a small saucepan, place wine and saffron over high heat and reduce until 4 tablespoons liquid remain. Set aside.

In a large skillet, heat butter over high heat. Season shrimp and fish pieces with creole seasoning and place them in hot butter. Cook 2–3 minutes. Turn shrimp and fish pieces and continue to cook for 3–5 more minutes. Add garlic. Sauté another 3 minutes. Add crabmeat, crawfish meat, and green onions, and cook until the crab is heated. Add saffron glaze and remove from heat. Add beurre blanc, salt, and black pepper.

On serving plates, arrange the shrimp around the outer areas of the plate. Place one eggplant wheel down and top with some of the seafood mixture. Continue to stack wheels, alternating with seafood. Distribute sauce evenly and serve immediately.

Yield: 6 servings

Grilled Tuna with Orange Ginger Butter Sauce

6 tuna steaks, 6 ounces each
¼ cup olive oil
1 tablespoon Crescent City Grill Creole Seasoning
12 shrimp, large
2 teaspoons Old Bay Seasoning
½ pound jumbo lump crabmeat
2 tablespoons white wine
2 tablespoons green onion, chopped
12 asparagus spears, lightly blanched
1½ cups **Ginger-Soy Butter Sauce (p. 120)**
1 red onion, shaved into very thin rings
1 cup **Seasoned Flour (p. 107)**
cottonseed oil, for deep-frying

Prepare the onions. Preheat the cottonseed oil to 350". Lightly dust the onions with the seasoned flour. Drop the onions in small batches into the oil and fry until crisp and golden brown. Remove and drain. These may be done an hour in advance and held in a dry, warm place.

Lightly oil tuna steaks with olive oil and season with creole seasoning. Cook on a grill over medium to high heat to medium rare. While tuna cooks, heat remaining oil over high heat. Season the shrimp with Old Bay Seasoning and sauté until pink. Add crabmeat, green onions, and deglaze with wine. When the tuna is just about done, season the asparagus and grill until it is warm. To serve, place a small pile of fried onions on each serving dish. Lay tuna on the onion. Ladle about 1½ ounces of sauce over the tuna steak and top with shrimp and crab. Garnish each one with 2 asparagus spears.

Yield: 6 servings

Eggplant Bayou Teche

12 eggplant rounds
1 cup **Seasoned Flour (p. 107)**
1½ cups **Eggwash (p. 107)**
1½ cups seasoned breadcrumbs
cottonseed oil, for deep-frying eggplant
16 large shrimp, peeled and deveined
1 tablespoon Crescent City Grill Creole Seasoning
3 ounces **Clarified Butter (p.107)**
2 tablespoons garlic, minced
¾ cup green onions, sliced
2 ounces white wine
1 pound jumbo lump crabmeat, picked of all shell
6 ounces **Beurre Blanc (p. 112)**

Peel eggplant and cut into round discs, about the circumference of a mayonnaise jar top and ¼ inch thick. Marinate eggplant in salted lemon ice water until ready to cook.

To fry eggplant rounds, dust them with seasoned flour, shake off excess flour, dip them in the eggwash, and coat with breadcrumbs. Fry a few at a time at 350° until medium brown and crispy. Be careful not to overload the oil. Drain on paper towels.

Season shrimp with creole seasoning and sauté in clarified butter until they become opaque. Add garlic and green onions, and cook for 2 minutes. Deglaze the pan with white wine. Add crabmeat and sauté another 2 minutes. Add beurre blanc. Place 3 eggplant rounds each on 4 plates and divide seafood mixture over the top of the eggplant rounds. Garnish with lemon and freshly chopped parsley.

Yield: 4 servings

"Happy and successful cooking doesn't rely only on know-how; it comes from the heart, makes great demands on the palate and needs enthusiasm and a deep love of food to bring it to life."—Georges Blanc

Beef, Chicken, Pork

Ribeye Steaks with Green Peppercorn Sauce

Roquefort Tenderloin

Peppered Beef Tenderloin with Mustard Cognac Sauce

Rack of Lamb with Raspberry Mint Sauce

Veal Anna

Chicken and Wild Rice

Stir-Fry Chicken

Basin Street Chicken

Zydeco Chicken

Greek Chicken

Chicken Marsala

Merlot Duck

Grilled Italian Sausage with Mushroom Risotto

State Inspected

This bovine beauty displays
her southernness for those
who can see it.

Ribeye Steaks with Green Peppercorn Sauce

Roquefort Tenderloin

"Cooking is at once one of the simplest and most gratifying of the arts, but to cook well one must love and respect food."
—Craig Claiborne

6 ribeye steaks
kosher salt
freshly ground black pepper
Crescent City Grill Steak Seasoning
½ cup shallots, chopped
4 ounces **Clarified Butter (p. 107)**
1 tablespoon garlic, minced
3 tablespoons green peppercorns
¼ cup brandy
1 cup demiglace
½ cup whipping cream

Preheat oven to 450°. Heat clarified butter in a large skillet over very high heat. Liberally season the steaks with kosher salt, black pepper, and steak seasoning. When butter is very hot, sear the steaks on both sides. Place browned steaks on a baking sheet and place them in the oven. Reduce heat under skillet and pour off all but 2 tablespoons of the butter. When skillet has cooled, add shallots and garlic and sauté quickly. Do not let garlic get too dark. Add peppercorns and deglaze with brandy. Allow brandy to reduce by one-half. Add demiglace and bring to a simmer for 1–2 minutes, then add cream. Bring to a simmer once again and allow sauce to cook for 4–5 more minutes. Turn off heat. When meat has reached desired doneness, place on serving dishes and spoon sauce over top.

If you prefer to grill your steaks, cut back on the amount of butter in the recipe; you will only need 1–2 teaspoons to cook the shallots, garlic, and peppercorns to make the sauce.

Yield: 6 servings

6 8-ounce beef tenderloin filets
3 tablespoons Crescent City Grill Steak Seasoning
3 ounces **Clarified Butter (p. 107)**
3 ounces brandy
2 tablespoons shallots, small dice
1 cup veal demiglace
4 ounces Roquefort or bleu cheese crumbles
¼ cup heavy cream

Preheat oven to 450°. In a large skillet, heat butter over high heat. Season filets liberally with steak seasoning. Place filets in skillet 3 at a time and sear both sides. Repeat with the remaining 3 steaks. Place browned filets on a baking sheet and place in oven. Turn down the heat on the skillet to low medium. Add shallots and sauté 1–2 minutes. Deglaze with brandy. Stir well and add demiglace. Add half of the cheese. Add cream and continue to stir well, cooking 4–5 minutes longer. Remove from heat. When filets have reached medium rare, sprinkle remaining cheese on top and allow cheese to melt slightly. Place filets on 6 individual plates and top with equal amounts of the sauce.

Yield: 6 servings

Peppered Beef Tenderloin with Mustard Cognac Sauce

Rack of Lamb with Raspberry Mint Sauce

6 beef tenderloin filets, 6-8 ounces each
kosher salt, to taste
½ cup black pepper, cracked
2 tablespoons **Clarified Butter (p. 107)**
1 cup heavy cream
½ cup demiglace
1 cup Half-n-Half
½ cup cognac
3 egg yolks
1 tablespoon flour
¼ cup dry mustard
2 tablespoons sugar
1 tablespoon cornstarch
1 tablespoon water
1 tablespoon apple cider vinegar
2 tablespoons Dijon mustard

Preheat oven to 425°. Season filets generously with kosher salt and press the cracked black pepper into the meat. In a large skillet, heat the clarified butter and sear filets on both sides. Place browned filets on a baking sheet and place in the oven. Heat the demiglace, cream, Half-n-Half and cognac in a medium sauce pot until it starts to simmer. In a mixing bowl, whip egg yolks. Temper them by slowly adding a small amount of the hot cream mixture. Then, add the yolk mixture back into the sauce pot. Do not boil! Mix together flour, sugar, and dry mustard and stir it into the hot cream. Dissolve the cornstarch in the water and add it to the cream. Bring back to a simmer and remove from heat. Stir in vinegar and Dijon mustard and hold in a warm place until ready to serve. When meat has reached desired doneness, place filets on serving dishes and spoon sauce over top.

Yield: 6 servings

1 cup fresh or frozen raspberries
½ cup sugar
1 cup red wine
6 lamb racks, domestic, 12–14 ounces each
3 tablespoons olive oil
kosher salt
freshly ground black pepper to taste
2 tablespoons shallot, minced
1½ cups veal demiglace
3 tablespoons butter, cold and cut into small pieces
3 tablespoons fresh mint leaves, chopped fine

In a saucepan over medium heat, combine raspberries, sugar, and red wine and simmer until most of the liquid is gone. Purée remaining mixture and pass through a fine mesh strainer to remove seeds. Set aside.

Preheat oven to 400°. Generously season lamb with kosher salt and black pepper. Heat olive oil in a large skillet over high heat. Sear lamb on both sides. Once the racks are brown, place them on a baking sheet and place in the oven.

Drain excess oil from the pan and add the shallot. Cook over low heat for 1–2 minutes. Add raspberry mixture and demiglace to the skillet. Bring to a simmer and let cook for 1–2 more minutes. Slowly, add butter pieces stirring constantly until thoroughly incorporated. Stir in mint. Remove sauce from heat. Once lamb has reached desired doneness, remove from oven and let it rest for 5–7 minutes. Cut lamb into 2-bone sections (1-bone chop if using large racks) and arrange on serving plates. Drizzle sauce over the chops. Serve with **Wild Mushroom Risotto (p. 93)**.

Yield: 6 servings

"An apple is an excellent thing—until you have tried a peach."—George du Maurier

Veal Anna

12 3-ounce veal medallions, pounded thin
1½ cups **Seasoned Flour (p. 107)**
½ to ¾ cup olive oil
12 large shrimp
1 teaspoon salt
½ teaspoon pepper
½ pound jumbo lump crabmeat
½ teaspoon garlic, minced
¼ cup white wine
juice of 1 lemon
1½ cups fresh cleaned spinach
1 tablespoon shallots, finely minced
1 teaspoon salt
½ teaspoon fresh ground black pepper
1 tablespoon parsley, chopped fine
1 recipe **Choron Sauce (p. 111)**

Preheat oven to 250°.

Lightly dredge the veal in the seasoned flour. In a large skillet place enough olive oil to coat the bottom. Place the skillet on high heat. When the oil is hot, brown the medallions. Be careful not to overload the skillet or the medallions will not brown. After browning each side, place them on a baking sheet. This procedure may need to be repeated several times depending on the size of the skillet. Once the medallions are all browned, place them in the oven.

Once again place a large skillet on a high heat and add enough oil to coat the bottom. Season the shrimp with 1 teaspoon salt and ½ teaspoon pepper. Sauté them for 3–4 minutes until they turn pink. Add the garlic and sauté for another 30–40 seconds; then add the crab, white wine, and lemon juice. Cook until crab is heated through and remove from heat. Keep in a warm place.

In a large mixing bowl combine the spinach with 1 teaspoon salt, ½ teaspoon pepper, and ¼ cup olive oil. Spread spinach mixture onto a baking sheet and place it in the oven. Just as it begins to wilt (do not let it wilt completely), remove and divide it into nice mounds in the center of your serving dishes. Next place the veal over the top of the spinach, 2 medallions per person. Spoon the choron sauce over the veal medallions and top with the shrimp and crab. Garnish with chopped parsley.

Yield: 6 servings

Chicken and Wild Rice

¼ cup **Clarified Butter (p. 107)**
2 cups mushrooms, sliced
½ cup red peppers, diced
½ cup green bell peppers, diced
½ cup yellow onion, small dice
2 tablespoons garlic, minced
2 pounds chicken, seasoned, cooked and diced
1 cup **Stir-Fry Sauce (p. 117)**
6 cups wild rice, cooked
6 pineapple slices
fresh parsley

In a large skillet, heat butter over high heat and sauté mushrooms until tender. Add peppers, onion, and garlic. Cook for 3–4 more minutes. Add rice. Add chicken and stir-fry sauce and heat thoroughly. Cook pineapple slices on a hot grill, or sear them until golden brown in a hot skillet. Garnish with pineapple and chopped parsley.

   Yield: 6 servings

Stir-Fry Chicken

2 pounds chicken breast, grilled and chopped into ½-inch
   pieces
3 tablespoons **Clarified Butter (p. 107)**
1 carrot, peeled and julienned
1 bunch broccoli, cut into small florettes
1 cup mushrooms
1 zucchini, julienned
1 summer squash, julienned
1 red pepper, seeds removed and julienned
1 tablespoon garlic, minced
¼ cup **Chicken Stock (p. 126)**
1½ cups **Stir-Fry Sauce (p. 117)**
8 cups white rice, cooked

Heat clarified butter in a large heavy skillet over high heat. Place carrots in butter first and cook for 2–3 minutes, stirring once or twice to keep from browning. Add mushrooms and broccoli and cook 3–4 minutes. Add chicken, zucchini, squash, peppers, and garlic. Stir the mixture constantly and cook 3 minutes. Add chicken stock and reduce by half. Add stir-fry sauce. Toss thoroughly and remove from heat. Divide heated rice onto serving dishes and divide stir-fry over rice.

   Yield: 6–8 servings

"Life expectancy would grow by leaps and bounds if green vegetables smelled as good as bacon."—Doug Larson

The Great Summer Squash Crisis

America is filled with movements. The women's movement, the civil rights movement, the conservative movement, the labor movement, and even the Lutheran student movement. I am the idiot who joined the Garden-To-The-Table-Movement.

To belong to the Garden-To-The-Table-Movement a restaurateur must grow or raise a portion of his menu offerings. I first learned of this movement in 1999 while attending a flavor dynamics seminar at the Culinary Institute of America in Napa Valley, California.

The CIA cultivates a majority of the vegetables used at their facility. The difference in flavor due to the freshness and quality of the product is unmistakable.

To start the day my classmates and I would venture into the CIA's meticulously manicured gardens to carefully select vegetables that were needed for that day's menu. There was something romantic about walking among the dew-covered produce in the morning garden with the cool California sunrise as a backdrop.

What a great idea, I thought. It's only seeds and dirt. People grow food in Mississippi all the time. I see them at the farmers' market. I pass those farms in my car. It couldn't be too hard. In addition to being a restaurateur and a chef, I could be a planter.

The word planter has always sounded so noble and refined. I knew friends in college whose parents were "Delta planters." Yes, I would be a planter—a Piney Woods planter.

Armed with a fool's determination, an idiot's resolve, and the *Farmer's Almanac,* I planted a two-acre garden at my farm outside of town.

Two acres didn't seem like a lot of garden at the time. I had passed plantations in the Delta that spanned thousands of acres. Certainly a determined and refined Piney Woods planter could manage a couple of measly acres in between lunch and dinner shifts at three different restaurants.

Squash was the first crop to come in.

Who knew that eight or nine 100-foot rows of seeds would produce so much? The first picking in my little experiment with the Garden-To-The-Table-Movement yielded seventeen bushels of squash. I picked them all myself. There weren't any classmates from

Nothing is more wholesome than fresh produce. The yellow squash against the purple eggplant are magnetic to the eye.

watters

the CIA offering to help. There was no cool California sunrise. It was hot and humid. Let me state emphatically that there was nothing romantic about it.

The Great Summer Squash Crisis of 2000 had begun.

Every cooler in the restaurant, including the beer cooler, was filled with squash. We prepared squash as the vegetable of the day, cream of squash soup, stuffed squash, fried squash, squash appetizers, squash salad, and squash surprise. We tried everything short of squash ice cream, and we were on the verge of trying that.

I picked twelve bushels of squash on the second day. By the third day, everyone I knew, and their relatives, had a refrigerator full of squash. On the fourth day of the Great Summer Squash Crisis, those so-called friends weren't returning my calls. They wouldn't even answer the door when I came to their houses. I resorted to ringing their doorbells, leaving bushels of squash on the doorstep, and running away. The Piney Woods Planter's dash!

By the time the other vegetables in my garden started coming in, I was in the process of opening two new restaurants. I couldn't keep up. The garden became overgrown and eventually went to seed. Today, a well-fertilized group of weeds is all that remains of my foray into the Garden-To-The-Table-Movement.

I am here to tell you, and this is coming from someone with twenty-two years in the restaurant business, farming is hard work. My Piney Woods planter's days are over. Nowadays, I don't even have a tomato plant in a clay pot on my back porch. From now on, I'll be getting my squash from the farmers' market.

· · ·

Recipe inspiration comes from many different places. In the case of baked shrimp and squash, the Garden-To-The-Table-Movement was the source. A walk-in cooler filled with seventeen bushels of squash tends to motivate one to think creatively.

Baked shrimp and squash is a recipe we still serve at lunch in the Purple Parrot Café (see page 45). It is perfect served at home as a quick and easy summer lunch for company, especially when served with a light tossed salad. It can be made the day before and refrigerated or a week ahead of time and frozen.

Basin Street Chicken

6 boneless, skinless chicken breasts, seasoned and grilled
2 tablespoons **Clarified Butter (p. 107)**
2 cups mushrooms, thinly sliced
1½ cups fresh tomato, medium dice
¼ cup white wine
1 teaspoon salt
½ teaspoon black pepper
1 cup **Caramelized Onions (p. 101)**
6 slices cheddar cheese
6 slices jack cheese
¼ cup fresh chopped parsley

Preheat oven to 400°.

Arrange grilled chicken breasts on a baking sheet. In a large skillet heat butter over high heat. Sauté mushrooms until they become tender. Add tomatoes, wine, and seasoning and reduce slightly. Add the caramelized onions and spoon mixture evenly over the chicken breasts. Top each chicken with a slice of both the cheddar and jack cheese. Place chicken in oven and heat until the cheese is melted. Place on serving dishes and top with parsley

Yield: 6 servings

Zydeco Chicken

6 boneless, skinless chicken breasts, seasoned and grilled
2 tablespoons **Clarified Butter (p. 107)**
½ pound andouille sausage, medium dice
1 tablespoon fresh garlic, minced
1½ cups **Creole Cream Sauce (p. 113)**
½ cup freshly grated Romano cheese
¼ cup freshly chopped parsley

In a large skillet heat the butter over high heat. Sauté the sausage for 2–3 minutes. Add the garlic and mushrooms and continue to cook for 6–7 minutes until mushrooms start to become tender. Deglaze with white wine and allow wine to reduce. Add green onions and creole cream sauce. When the sauce is thoroughly heated, stir in the Romano cheese and allow sauce to thicken slightly. Spoon over the grilled chicken and garnish with the chopped parsley.

Yield: 6 servings

"These things are just plain annoying. After all the trouble you go to, you get about as much actual 'food' out of eating an artichoke as you would from licking 30 or 40 postage stamps. Have the shrimp cocktail instead."
—Miss Piggy

Greek Chicken

"Monsieur Guizot assures us that while he was ambassador in London, his cook was more useful to him politically than his secretaries."
—Lucien Tendret

4 chicken breasts, boneless, skinless
½ cup all-purpose flour
2 tablespoons Crescent City Grill Poultry Seasoning
⅓ cup vegetable oil or margarine
⅓ cup olive oil
⅔ cup shiitake mushrooms, sliced
⅔ cup portobello mushrooms, sliced
⅔ cup button mushrooms, sliced
4 tablespoons sun-dried tomatoes, sliced
2 tablespoons garlic minced
2 ounces white wine
3 cups fresh spinach, stemmed
¾ cup feta cheese, crumbled
salt and pepper, to taste
¾ cup **Beurre Blanc (p. 112)**

Preheat oven to 400°. Mix flour and poultry seasoning thoroughly. Heat vegetable oil or margarine in a sauté pan over medium-high heat. Dust chicken breasts in seasoned flour and shake off excess flour. Sauté in pan until lightly browned on both sides. Place chicken breasts on a sheet pan and cook in oven until done.

Chicken breasts can also be grilled. Skip the flour, and season the chicken with the poultry seasoning. Grill breasts until done. Set aside.

In a separate sauté pan, heat olive oil. Add mushrooms and sun-dried tomatoes. Cook until mushrooms are soft. Add garlic and stir. Deglaze pan with white wine. Add spinach and stir until wilted. Add cheese, salt, and pepper. Remove from heat and add beurre blanc.

Place the chicken breasts on four separate plates. Spoon the topping on the chicken breasts. Serve hot.

Yield: 4 servings

Chicken Marsala

6 chicken breasts, boneless, skinless
1 cup all purpose flour
2 tablespoons Crescent City Grill Poultry Seasoning
⅓ cup oil or margarine
⅓ cup **Clarified Butter (p. 107)**
3 cups mushrooms, sliced
2 tablespoons Garlic
2 cups artichoke hearts, quartered
1 tablespoon Crescent City Grill Creole Seasoning
½ cup Marsala wine
1 cup **Beurre Blanc (p. 112)**

Preheat oven to 400°.

Mix flour and seasoning thoroughly. Heat oil in a sauté pan over medium high heat. Lightly dust chicken breasts in seasoned flour and shake off excess flour. Sauté in pan until lightly browned on both sides. Place chicken breasts on a sheet pan and place in the oven until cooked through.

In a separate sauté pan heat clarified butter. Add mushrooms and sauté until tender. Add garlic, artichoke hearts, and creole seasoning. Deglaze with Marsala wine. Remove from heat and add beurre blanc. Stir to incorporate.

Place each of the chicken breasts on one of six serving plates. Evenly distribute the Marsala topping on top of the six breasts. Spoon any sauce remaining in pan over chicken. Serve immediately.

Yield: 6 servings

Merlot Duck

1 cup balsamic vinegar
¼ cup merlot wine
½ cup brown sugar
¾ cup demiglace
1 tablespoon Crescent City Grill Cayenne and Garlic Sauce
6 duck breasts, boneless
kosher salt, to taste
fresh ground black pepper, to taste
1 recipe **Roasted Sweet Potatoes (p. 100)**
¼ pound **Crispy Fried Prosciutto (p. 92)**

Preheat oven to 400°. In a heavy saucepan, combine the first 5 ingredients. Bring to a low simmer and reduce by one-third. Watch sauce carefully as it can burn easily. Once reduced, remove the sauce from heat and hold in a warm place.

Using a sharp knife, score the fat side of the duck breast by cutting shallow X's into the skin. Season both sides of the breasts with kosher salt and fresh ground pepper. Heat a large skillet over medium heat and place breasts fat side down in skillet. Allow to cook on the fat side for about 6–7 minutes. Turn the heat up to high and sear the other side of the breasts. Remove from skillet and place on a baking sheet fat side up. Brush the fat side of the duck with the merlot glaze. Bake breasts in the oven to medium doneness (3–5 minutes). Remove the duck from the oven and allow it to rest for 5 minutes in a warm area.

Arrange a serving of sweet potatoes in the center of each serving dish. Slice the duck breast and arrange around the potatoes. Drizzle the remaining glaze over the duck and top the duck with the crispy fried prosciutto.

Yield: 6 servings

Grilled Italian Sausage with Mushroom Risotto

3 pounds Italian sausage
1 tablespoon Crescent City Grill Creole Seasoning
1 recipe **Wild Mushroom Risotto (p. 93)**
½ cup Parmesan cheese, freshly grated

Prepare gas or charcoal grill to medium heat. Split sausage lengthwise and season with creole seasoning. Place sausage on grill and cook thoroughly. Serve with mushroom risotto. Garnish with freshly grated Parmesan cheese and freshly chopped parsley.

Yield: 6–8 servings

"I like a cook who smiles out loud when he tastes his own work. Let God worry about your modesty; I want to see your enthusiasm."
—Robert Farrar Capon

Pig Farming

After my disappointments and misadventures in the Garden-To-The-Table movement, and my lack of proficiency in vegetable gardening, I searched for a new food-related hobby; I decided to give pig farming a try.

Pigs had to be easier to grow than vegetables. I wouldn't have to use a tiller, and, like me, pigs eat almost anything. So, to my wife's dismay, I bought some pigs.

The guy I bought them from said they were Yorkshire pigs. That sounded very noble and refined. I could see myself owning a Yorkshire pig. Maybe they would be shipped all the way from a country estate in Northern England. Yes, they would be blue-blooded pigs.

It turns out these noble blue-blooded pigs did not come from Yorkshire County, England, but from Perry County, Mississippi, just south of Hattiesburg. They were far from being refined. They had been rolling around in something that looked, but didn't smell like, Yorkshire pudding. They smelled like most British food tastes.

The pig salesman pulled up in my driveway early one Saturday morning. We knew he was there, not because he honked his horn or rang the doorbell, but because we could smell the pigs from inside the house.

My daughter ran outside to see the pigs. There were three of them. She said they looked just like Babe from the Hollywood movie *Babe, Pig in the City*. It was at that moment that I knew the future of ham, bacon, sausage, and ribs at my dinner table could be in jeopardy. Before long, the four year old would be naming the pigs, traveling to the farm to visit her new pets, dressing them up, and putting bows and ribbons on their heads.

I know nothing about pig farming or raising pigs. The extent of my porcine knowledge comes from cooking with andouille sausage, listening to the Pink Floyd album *Animals* and watching Arnold, Mr. Ziffle's pig, on *Green Acres*.

One of my pigs was a dead ringer for Arnold, the *Green Acres* pig. Who knew Arnold was a Yorkshire? Arnold the pig came to Hattiesburg when I was a boy. He was the headliner at the Great South Fair. He solved complicated math equations by grunting the answers. Arnold could also count to twelve when his handler prodded him with a stick. None of the pigs in the back of the truck looked smart enough to do anything like that.

Running in Place

Chimneyville Smokehouse serves up barbeque plates and has a kiddy ride with a twist—in the tail that is. It is not a horse that you feed quarters but a pig.

My friend Banks Norman owned the farm where we would house and feed the pigs. He would run the piggery. This was not Banks's first venture into the pig farming business. He had two pigs a few years ago. His kids named them (a sure sign of trouble). They were called Porkchop and Hambone, two things he was not going to be getting from his pigs.

Banks raised the pigs in a dog pen with his border collies. The pigs grew up with the dogs. Before long, Porkchop and Hambone thought they were dogs. When anyone pulled in his driveway, both of the 300-pound pigs ran over, jumped up on their car, and stuck their snouts in the window.

Banks had to give Porkchop and Hambone away. His children wouldn't let him take them to the slaughterhouse, and the United States Postal Service didn't appreciate it when they started chasing the mailman.

My wife and I drove our new pigs out to the newly established piggery. They were put in a pen next to the dogs, not with the dogs. Luckily, I escaped the whole ordeal without my daughter naming them.

As the pig salesman drove off, he yelled out his window "You will need to castrate the pigs."

I turned to my wife and said, "Excuse me dear, did he say I was going to have to refrigerate the pigs?"

"No. He said you were going to have to castrate the pigs," she said, with a smile.

"When pigs fly," I said.

My wife just laughed.

I didn't know I was getting involved in anything that could make a pig cry wee, wee, wee all the way home.

A few days later, one of my lead line cooks volunteered to come out to the piggery and do the deed. When he got out of his truck, I noticed that he wasn't carrying any sterilized surgical instruments or one of those black leather house call bags. All he had in his hands were an old and well-worn pocketknife, a few rubber bands, and some used axle grease. I'll leave the gory details to the reader's imagination.

As it turns out, the dog pen was perfect for containing one medium-sized herding dog, but it was no match for three 200-pound Yorkshire pigs. The pigs escaped easily and often. The good news is that they were easy to find. The bad news is that they were usually in the neighbor's garden.

I had always heard that pigs are smart, and that is true. But they are devious too. Banks worked on Thursday, Friday, and Saturday nights. Somehow, the pigs knew this. The only nights that they ever made a break for it were weekend nights while he was at work.

I had no idea pigs smelled so bad. I am at a loss as I search for a descriptive and comparable odor that would explain the degree of stench that emanated from that pigpen. There is really no other odor on the planet that comes close to that of a crowded pigpen on a hot Mississippi August afternoon. If the wind was right, you could smell it 300 yards down the road. For the record, I would like my mother to know once and for all, that as a kid my room might have looked like a pigsty, but it never smelled like one.

We agreed to wait until the pigs reached 300 pounds before taking them to the meat processor, but Banks was in the process of selling his house, and having three big, smelly pigs wallowing around in his side yard didn't make for viable and marketable real estate. The wife and kids had also had enough.

The pigs knew something was up as he loaded them onto the trailer for their final journey. They attacked him and ate part of the left leg of his Levi's.

I received a call from the meat packing plant informing me that the pigs were ready to be processed. "Do you want smoked or fresh?" the man asked.

"Smoked or fresh what?" I replied.

"Sausage and bacon," he said, forgetting to add "you idiot!" on the end of his comeback.

It is amazing how much pork comes from one 200-pound pig. When I opened the bags of pork I was astonished to find what seemed like hundreds of pork chops, patty sausages, and a year's supply of bacon.

As I dug deeper into my sack-o-swine, I got the eerie feeling that someone was watching me. After moving a package of link sausage to one side, that intuition proved true. And there it was—a pig's head! That's right, the whole head—looking right back at me—eyes, snout, and all. It was my pig's head, and he didn't look too happy either. It was a sight that could turn a steadfast and devoted carnivore into a card-carrying vegetarian.

The feet were in the bag also, along with the liver, tail, heart, small pieces of lard, and assorted and sundry bones and joints. The more I dug into the bags the meat processor gave me, the more parts I found. I think if I had looked hard enough, I probably would have found the long-lost baby blue sock that matched the powder-blue leisure suit I wore back in 1976.

As luck would have it, some of my cooks at the restaurant fought over who would get the head, feet, and organs. Headcheese and souse are two things I can do without.

I had always heard the culinary term "headcheese," but I was never quite sure what it was. I was so naïve in the ways of the hog that I thought "souse" was just a thick-drawled South Mississippi mispronunciation of the word "sauce." Think again, chef boy. As I understand it, to make headcheese or souse you take the pig's ears, snout, feet, heart, tail, and the whole head and boil them in a pot with salt, pepper, and vinegar. Yummy, where do I sign up! This is supposed to be a tasty treat when sliced and placed on top of a soda cracker.

For an extra treat, I was told that cleaned chitlins (intestines) could be placed in a cloth feed bag and boiled alongside the other souse ingredients. Double yummy! "But, make sure and keep them separated," they say. God knows we need to keep those pesky intestines away from the clean and untainted head and snout.

After my brief stint in the pig farming business, I think I'll take one more stab at vegetable gardening. My pig-farming days were over, just five short months after they began.

Shucks

This corn roaster at the State Fair has to wear gloves to beat the heat. This may be the only truly healthful eating to be had at what is an otherwise deep-fried event.

Pasta

Mardi Gras Pasta

Pasta Jambalaya

Shrimp Pasta with Basil, Corn, and Tomatoes

Fettuccine Alfredo

Three Cheese Tortellini

BBQ Shrimp Pasta

Chicken and Pesto Pasta

Chicken and Andouille Fettuccine

Kings and Queens

Elvis has not left the building at Hal and Mal's. He hangs around the bathroom. Chenilles of the King are now quite collectible since the estate has put a clamp on the name and visage.

Mardi Gras Pasta

Pasta Jambalaya

2 pounds shrimp, 31–35 count, peeled and deveined
2 tablespoons Crescent City Grill Creole Seasoning
4 ounces **Clarified Butter (p. 107)**
½ cup green bell pepper, small dice
½ cup red bell pepper, small dice
½ cup onion, small dice
1½ cups tomato, chopped
2 tablespoons garlic, minced
1 pound crawfish tails
1¾ cups **Parmesan Cream Sauce (p. 117)**
1 cup heavy whipping cream
1 pound fettuccine

Cook the fettuccine in boiling water to al dente. Sprinkle shrimp with 2 teaspoons of the creole seasoning. In a heavy sauté pan over medium high heat, add the clarified butter, bell peppers, and onion. Cook for 1 minute. Add the seasoned shrimp. When the vegetables begin to get soft and the shrimp turn pink, add the tomatoes and crawfish. When crawfish are heated through, add the Parmesan cream sauce and remaining 2 teaspoons of creole seasoning, stirring well. Add the heavy whipping cream and stir well to blend with the sauce. Cook for 3 to 4 minutes until sauce has reduced and become thick. Divide pasta among 6 plates and top with seafood mixture making sure that each portion gets 4 shrimp and an equal amount of crawfish.

Yield: 6 servings

3 tablespoons **Clarified Butter (p. 107)**
¾ pound andouille sausage, medium dice
½ cup red bell pepper, small dice
½ cup green bell pepper, small dice
½ cup red onion, small dice
2 tablespoons garlic, minced
1 pound grilled chicken, medium dice
2 cups mushrooms, thinly sliced
1½ cups **Crescent City Grill Creole Sauce (p. 110)**
1 cup **Parmesan Cream Sauce (p. 117)**
½ cup heavy cream
1 pound crawfish tails
1 pound dry pasta, cooked to al dente*
¼ cup chopped parsley
½ cup freshly grated Parmesan cheese

In a large skillet heat the butter over high heat. Sauté sausage, peppers, and onion for 3–4 minutes, just until peppers start to become tender. Add the garlic, chicken, and mushrooms and continue to cook for 6–7 minutes. Add the creole sauce, Parmesan cream sauce, and cream. Lower the heat to medium. Add the crawfish. Stir sauces to incorporate thoroughly and allow to simmer for 3–4 minutes until desired thickness is achieved. Toss with the cooked pasta and divide into serving dishes. Garnish with parsley and Parmesan.

* We use a combination of fusilli, penne, and bowtie pasta. You can use whatever you like, but should start with 1 pound of dry pasta. If you are using smaller pastas, you may want to increase the weight by about 20 percent.

Yield: 6 servings

Shrimp Pasta with Basil, Corn, and Tomatoes

2 pounds shrimp, 31–35 count, peeled and deveined
1 tablespoon Old Bay Seasoning
¼ cup olive oil
½ cup white wine
2 cups **Tomato Concasse (p. 107)**
2 cups corn, fresh cut or frozen
¾ cup **Pesto (p. 113)**
¼ cup butter, unsalted and softened
1 teaspoon salt
1 teaspoon fresh black pepper
1 pound fettuccine
½ cup basil, freshly chopped

In a large mixing bowl, combine corn, tomatoes, and pesto. Allow this to marinate for 1–2 hours.

Cook the fettuccine in boiling water to al dente and set aside.

Season shrimp with Old Bay Seasoning. Heat oil in a large skillet over high heat. Once oil is very hot, place shrimp in skillet. Once shrimp begin to turn pink (1–2 minutes), move them around in the skillet and cook for another 2-3 minutes. Deglaze with white wine and allow wine to reduce by half. Stir in pesto mixture and season with salt and pepper. Once mixture is thoroughly hot, add softened butter and allow it to melt and mix with the sauce. Add cooked pasta and serve. Garnish with fresh chopped parsley.

Yield: 6 servings

Fettuccine Alfredo

1 tablespoon olive oil
1 tablespoon garlic, minced
2 cups heavy whipping cream
2 cups **Parmesan Cream Sauce (p.117)**
½ cup Parmesan cheese, freshly grated
¼ cup parsley, freshly chopped
1 pound fettuccine

Cook the fettuccine in boiling water to al dente and set aside.

In a large skillet or sauce pot, heat oil over medium heat and sweat the garlic for 1–2 minutes, being careful not to let it brown. Add heavy cream and bring to a low simmer. Add cream sauce and, using a wire whip, incorporate the two. Bring sauce back up to a simmer and allow it to cook until it reaches desired thickness. Once it has reached desired consistency, add pasta. Coat all noodles and place into serving dishes. Garnish with Parmesan cheese and freshly chopped parsley.

Yield: 6 servings

"Nature will castigate those who don't masticate."
—Horace (chew your food 32 times) Fletcher

Three Cheese Tortellini

2 tablespoons **Clarified Butter (p. 107)**
1½ cups sliced mushrooms
2 tablespoons fresh garlic, minced
¾ cup red bell pepper, small dice
¾ cup green bell pepper, small dice
½ cup red onion, small dice
1 cup sun-dried tomatoes
2 teaspoons salt
1 teaspoon black pepper
2 pounds grilled chicken, medium dice
½ cup white wine
½ cup **Parmesan Cream Sauce (p. 117)**
1½ cups heavy cream
3 tablespoons fresh basil, rough chop
2 pounds fresh cheese tortellini, cooked until tender
¼ cup Parmesan cheese

Heat butter in a large skillet over medium-high heat. Sauté mushrooms and garlic for 4–5 minutes. Add the peppers, onions, and sun-dried tomatoes and cook for 2–3 more minutes. Add the chicken and deglaze with white wine. Allow wine to reduce. Add salt and pepper, Parmesan cream sauce, and cream. Incorporate the sauces thoroughly and allow to simmer until sauce reaches desired thickness. Add 2 tablespoons fresh basil and toss with the tortellini. Divide into serving dishes and top with remaining basil and Parmesan cheese.

Yield: 6 servings

BBQ Shrimp Pasta

¼ cup olive oil
1½ pounds large shrimp, 31–35 count, peeled and deveined
1½ cups **BBQ Shrimp Stock (p. 50)**
1 cup heavy cream
1½ cups **Parmesan Cream Sauce (p. 117)**
1 pound linguini
1 tablespoon black pepper, cracked
½ cup green onions, thinly sliced

Cook the linguini in boiling water to al dente and set aside.

In a large skillet, heat olive oil over high heat. Place shrimp in hot oil and sear. Cook shrimp 2–3 minutes. Add the BBQ shrimp stock and bring sauce to a simmer. Add cream and Parmesan cream sauce and reduce until thickened. Divide hot cooked pasta into 6 serving dishes and spoon sauce over noodles. Garnish with the cracked black pepper and sliced green onions.

Yield: 6 servings

Chicken and Pesto Pasta

3 tablespoons **Clarified Butter (p. 107)**
2 cups mushrooms, sliced
½ cup sun-dried tomatoes
½ cup black olives, sliced
½ cup white wine
2 pounds chicken, diced and cooked
1½ cups **Parmesan Cream Sauce (p. 117)**
1 cup heavy cream
¾ cup **Pesto (p. 113)**
1 teaspoon salt
⅓ teaspoon fresh black pepper
1 pound fettuccine
⅓ cup Parmesan cheese for garnish

Cook the fettuccini in boiling water to al dente and set aside.

Heat butter in a large skillet over high heat. Sauté mushrooms for 4–5 minutes until tender. Add sun-dried tomatoes, olives, and white wine. Reduce wine by half and add in chicken, Parmesan cream sauce, and heavy cream and bring to a simmer. Add salt, pepper, and pesto. Toss with cooked fettuccine and place on serving plates. Garnish with Parmesan cheese and parsley.

Yield: 6 servings

Chicken and Andouille Fettuccine

⅓ cup **Clarified Butter (p. 107)**
½ cup red bell pepper, medium dice
½ cup green bell pepper, medium dice
1 cup yellow onion, medium dice
1 pound andouille sausage, rough cut
3 tablespoons garlic, minced
2 cups mushrooms, sliced (shiitake or button)
1½ tablespoons Crescent City Grill Creole Seasoning
2 cups chicken breast, seasoned, grilled, and diced
2 cups **Creole Cream Sauce (p. 113)**
1 cup heavy cream
1 pound fettuccine

Cook the fettuccine in boiling water to al dente and set aside.

Heat clarified butter in a heavy sauté pan. Add peppers and onions. Cook until soft and translucent. Add andouille and stir well. Add garlic and mushrooms. Cook until mushrooms are soft. Add creole seasoning and cooked chicken, stirring well to incorporate. Add creole cream sauce stirring continuously until heated through. Add heavy cream to reach desired thickness. Once heated through, serve over heated fettuccine.

Yield: 6 servings

"The stomach is the center and origin of civilization."
—Unknown

Vegetables and Sides

Crispy Fried Prosciutto

Café Potatoes

Wild Mushroom Risotto

Ratatouille

Sufferin' Succotash

Apricot Casserole

Wasabi Basil Smashed Potatoes

Andouille Cheese Grits

Vegetable Stir-Fry

Spinach Gratin

Pesto Pasta Salad

Roasted Sweet Potatoes

Honey-Roasted Nuts

Caramelized Onions

Roasted Peppers

Red Pepper Coulis

Pizza Crusts

Seasoned Flour

Clarified Butter

Eggwash

Tomato Concasse

Sow's Purse, Silk Ear

An antique purse seemed to invite comparison with these husky beauties. It's corny, but there is a kernel of truth to every saying.

Crispy Fried Prosciutto

Café Potatoes

1 cup prosciutto, cut into long, matchstick-thin strips
cottonseed oil for frying

To fry the prosciutto, heat cottonseed oil to 350°. Drop the strips of prosciutto into the oil and fry for 30–40 seconds. Remove from oil and drain on a paper towel.

3 pounds new potatoes, quartered, skin-on
¼ cup butter
2 tablespoons Crescent City Grill Creole Seasoning
1 tablespoon fresh rosemary (chopped)

Steam or boil new potatoes to just before fork-tender and transfer immediately to refrigerator to cool. Hold cold until ready to cook. Fry new potatoes at 350° until golden brown. Toss with butter, seasoning, and rosemary.

Yield: 8–10 servings

Wild Mushroom Risotto

3 tablespoons + 2 tablespoons whole unsalted butter
2 cups Aborio rice
3 tablespoons shallots, minced
4–6 cups hot vegetable stock
1 tablespoon salt, added to the vegetable stock
¾ pound wild mushrooms (shiitakes, porcinis, morels, chanterelles, criminis, portobellos, oysters), cleaned and sliced
1 cup cream
½ cup Parmesan cheese, freshly grated
2 tablespoons fresh parsley, chopped
2 teaspoons fresh thyme, chopped
1 teaspoon fresh ground black pepper

In a very large skillet, heat 3 tablespoons of butter over medium heat and add shallots. Cook until onions become soft. Add rice. Stir constantly to prevent rice from browning. The grains of rice need to get hot. Add 1½ cups of stock and turn heat down so that the stock is just barely simmering. Continue to stir constantly. As the stock is absorbed, add more stock in small amounts. Continue this process until the grains have become slightly tender. In a separate skillet, place the other 2 tablespoons of butter over a medium heat. Add cleaned sliced mushrooms and sauté until soft. Add the mushrooms to the risotto. When rice is almost completely cooked, add the cream and again stir until the moisture is absorbed. Remove from heat and stir in cheese, pepper, and fresh herbs. Serve immediately.

Yield: 6–8 servings

Ratatouille

½ cup good quality extra virgin olive oil
¾ cup yellow onion, medium dice
2 tablespoons garlic, minced
1½ cups yellow squash, cut into ½-inch cubes
1½ cups zucchini, cut into ½-inch cubes
1½ cups eggplant, salted, rinsed, and cut into ½-inch cubes
1 teaspoon salt
1 cup red peppers, medium dice
2 teaspoons Crescent City Grill Creole Seasoning
1½ cups **Tomato Concasse (p. 107)**
¼ cup white wine
¾ cup fresh basil, chopped fine (do not substitute dried)

In a sauté pan over medium high heat, sweat onion in olive oil. Add garlic. Add next 5 ingredients and cook until vegetables become al dente. Add tomato concasse. Add salt and creole seasoning. Deglaze with wine and add basil at the very end, making sure to stir it in thoroughly without having it discolor too much. Cook 1–2 minutes.

Yield: 1½ quarts or 6–8 servings

"It is chief of this world's luxuries. . . . When one has tasted it, he knows what Angels eat. It was not a Southern watermelon that Eve took; we know it because she repented."—Mark Twain

Sufferin' Succotash

3 tablespoons olive oil
2 cups squash, medium dice
¼ cup onion, small chopped
1 red bell pepper, medium dice
1 cup fresh lima beans, cooked
1 cup corn kernels, freshly scraped
½ cup **Chicken Stock (p. 126)** or vegetable stock
2 teaspoons Crescent City Grill Creole Seasoning
2 teaspoons fresh thyme, chopped
½ teaspoon fresh rosemary, chopped
1 tablespoon butter
salt and pepper to taste

Heat olive oil over medium high heat. Add squash, onion, and bell pepper. Cook until softened. Add beans and corn and continue cooking 1–2 minutes. Add the stock. Reduce heat to low and simmer until almost all liquid has been evaporated. Add seasoning, herbs, and butter.

Yield: 6–8 servings

Apricot Casserole

3 16-ounce cans apricot halves, lightly drained
1 cup light brown sugar
1 stick unsalted butter, cut into pats
1½ sleeves Ritz crackers, crushed into small pieces almost to crumb state

Preheat oven to 350°. Grease a 2½-quart casserole dish. Using a bowl, crush the apricot halves between your fingers. Add the brown sugar and Ritz crackers and mix well. Pour mixture into the casserole dish and dot with the butter pats.

At the Purple Parrot, we add additional Ritz crackers and place all of the ingredients into greased individual gelatin molds. You might also want to use a tablespoon of lemon juice.

Yield: 8–10 servings

Wasabi Basil Smashed Potatoes

5 large Idaho potatoes, peeled and cut into even-sized large chunks
water to cover potatoes
2 tablespoons + 1 tablespoon salt
¼ pound cold unsalted butter, cut into 1-inch cubes
¼ cup wasabi powder dissolved in ¼ cup cold water
⅓ cup sour cream
¾ cup heavy cream, heated
3 tablespoons **Pesto (p. 113)**
¼ cup fresh parsley, chopped

Use the first 2 tablespoons of salt in the water to cook potatoes. Cook over medium heat until fork tender. Do not overcook; they will break up and absorb the water, resulting in a watery and less tasteful final product. Drain off all excess water and allow potatoes to sit in the dry, warm pot for 2 minutes. This will evaporate any excess moisture. Place potatoes in a mixing bowl. Using a whip attachment, begin to whip the potatoes on medium speed, breaking up the large pieces. Add butter cubes a few at a time and mix until well blended. Turn your mixer down to a low speed and add the wasabi, sour cream, and salt. Slowly pour in the hot cream. Fold in pesto and parsley just before serving.

Yield: 6–8 servings

Andouille Cheese Grits

1 tablespoon **Clarified Butter (p. 107)**
½ pound andouille sausage, medium dice
2 teaspoons garlic, minced
4 cups milk
1 teaspoon salt
¼ teaspoon cayenne pepper
2 tablespoons Crescent City Grill Cayenne and Garlic Sauce
2 tablespoons Crescent City Grill Creole Seasoning
½ cup unsalted butter
1 cup white grits, quick cooking
1 cup cheddar cheese, grated

In a large skillet, heat clarified butter until hot. Add andouille and garlic and sauté for 4–5 minutes. Remove from heat and drain off excess fat using a fine mesh strainer. Set aside.

In a large saucepan, bring the milk, seasonings, and butter to a boil. Slowly pour in grits while stirring constantly. Reduce heat to low. Continue to stir for 15 minutes. Add the sautéed andouille, garlic mix, and cheese. Serve immediately or to use for frying purposes, spread cheese grits onto a large baking sheet and chill.

Yield: 6–8 servings

"Vegetarianism is harmless enough, though it is apt to fill a man with wind and self-righteousness."
—Sir Robert Hutchinson

Easy Bake Oven

Christmas, 1966. Lyndon Johnson was president. *Time* magazine's man of the year wasn't a man at all (that year *Time* picked "the younger generation," eighteen to twenty-five year olds). Dr. Seuss's *How the Grinch Stole Christmas* was released for TV. The Beatles *Revolver* was the album of the year, and all I wanted for Christmas was an Easy Bake Oven. Not a football or a GI Joe or a new bike, but an Easy Bake Oven.

There it is. I've said it. After years of ribbing from friends and family, I can admit, without hesitation, that as a five-year-old boy I played with an Easy Bake Oven.

I remember that Christmas like it was yesterday. The oven was tall and metal and painted in that crazy blue-green color that was popular in the 1960s. The Easy Bake was outfitted with a 100-watt light bulb and all the miniature cookware needed to be a successful kindergarten chef. It was a blast. Some of my friends laughed and poked fun, but they were laughing with their mouths full as they never failed to line up and eat the cakes and cookies that came from the blue-green cooking machine.

Cut to Christmas, 2000. Bill Clinton was our president. *Time* magazine's man of the year was George W. Bush (a member of the younger generation the publication saluted in 1966). Ron Howard's *How the Grinch Stole Christmas* was a hit on the big screen. The Beatles held the number-one spot on the album charts, and my friend Chip Carey gave my three-year-old daughter an Easy Bake Oven.

The Easy Bake has seen many changes over the last thirty-four years. Instead of metal it was made with plastic. The wonderful blue-green color had been changed to white, and it was a little bit smaller than I remembered. But it still cooked with a 100-watt light bulb and it still offered a good time, in this case a memorable event for a father and a daughter.

It was one of the last presents my daughter opened on Christmas morning. She was eager to begin baking as soon as she opened the box, but we didn't have a 100-watt bulb in the house. After a quick trip to the twenty-four-hour drugstore and an even quicker look at the instructions (I at least glance at assembly instructions now that I'm almost an adult) she plugged it in. We made a yellow cake with chocolate icing. I can safely say that it was the highlight of my holidays.

Stovetop Stuff

We had an electric stove growing up, but when I went to visit my favorite aunt, I could smell the gas stove and know something was cooking.

That little cake was one of the best I had ever eaten. Not because of the quality of the Hasbro Toy Company's cake and icing. Not because of the size of the finished product (it could be eaten in three or four bites), but because of the sheer joy and complete adulation shown by my daughter as we made a miniature cake cooked by the heat of a light bulb at the foot of our Christmas tree on the floor of our den.

Maybe she has a future in the restaurant business. Who knows, it worked for me. Could it be too much to ask that she listen to and enjoy the Beatles?

Vegetable Stir-Fry

1 tablespoon olive oil
1 tablespoon unsalted butter
1 tablespoon shallots, finely minced
1 large zucchini, julienned
1 large summer squash, julienned
1 large carrot, peeled, julienned, and lightly blanched
1 red bell pepper, julienned
¼ cup **Chicken Stock (p. 126)**
salt and pepper

In a large skillet heat the olive oil over high heat. Then quickly add the whole butter and shallots. Stir the shallots for just a few seconds; then add the vegetables. Sauté them for 1–2 minutes, and then pour in the chicken stock. Allow the stock to reduce while stirring the vegetables. Season with salt and pepper and serve immediately.

 Yield: 6–8 servings

Spinach Gratin

2 tablespoons olive oil
2 tablespoons garlic, minced
1 cup whipping cream
1 cup **Parmesan Cream Sauce (p. 117)**
1 cup Parmesan cheese
2 tablespoons Crescent City Grill Cayenne and Garlic Sauce
1 tablespoon lemon juice
1 tablespoon Crescent City Grill Creole Seasoning
2 pounds spinach, frozen, thawed, and squeezed dry
10 ounces fresh spinach leaves, stems removed
2 teaspoons salt
½ teaspoon black pepper

In a large skillet, heat olive oil over medium heat and sauté garlic for 1–2 minutes, being careful not to brown. Add whipping cream and bring to a simmer. Let this cook down for 3–4 minutes. Whisk in Parmesan cream sauce. Continue to cook, reducing mixture until it becomes thick. Add seasonings. Place fresh spinach leaves and frozen spinach in a large bowl and pour hot mixture over spinach. Using a large spatula or spoon, stir well, incorporating the cream and the spinach. Return it to the skillet and cook for 5–6 more minutes, or until spinach is thoroughly heated. Serve immediately.

 Yield: 6 servings

"Tastes are made, not born."
—Mark Twain

Pesto Pasta Salad

"Laughter is brightest where food is best."—Irish Proverb

½ pound Rotini pasta (cooked, cooled, and slightly oiled to prevent it from sticking)
1½ cups tomato, remove seeds and small dice
½ cup green onion, chopped
½ cup toasted pinenuts
½ cup mayonnaise
½ cup sour cream
½ cup **Pesto (p. 113)**
2 teaspoons salt
2 teaspoons Crescent City Grill Cayenne and Garlic Sauce
3 tablespoons white balsamic vinegar
½ cup Parmesan cheese, freshly grated

Combine the mayonnaise, sour cream, pesto, vinegar, salt, and cayenne and garlic sauce to make the dressing. Toss the pasta with the dressing and gently fold in remaining ingredients. Refrigerate until ready to serve. Sprinkle with fresh Parmesan cheese to serve.

Yield: 6–8 servings (as a side salad)

Roasted Sweet Potatoes

3 pounds sweet potatoes, peeled and cut into 1½-inch cubes
1 cup melted butter
1 cup light brown sugar
2 teaspoons Crescent City Grill Cayenne and Garlic Sauce
2 teaspoons cinnamon

Preheat oven to 375°.

In a large saucepan, cover the sweet potatoes with cold water. Place the pan over medium heat and cook until potatoes become tender. (They will not take as long as you think.) Do not boil them. Gently drain the sweet potatoes in a colander. In a large mixing bowl combine the melted butter, brown sugar, cayenne and garlic sauce, and cinnamon. Gently fold in the potatoes so that they become evenly coated.

Spread the potatoes onto a lightly-oiled baking sheet and place in the oven for 20 minutes, or until golden brown. Remove from the oven and allow them to sit for 4–5 minutes before serving.

Yield: 6–8 servings

Honey-Roasted Nuts

½ cup **Clarified Butter (p. 107)**
½ cup sugar
1 cup slivered almonds
1 cup pecan pieces

In a large skillet or sauté pan heat butter and sugar together until the sugar is melted and starts to caramelize. Add the nuts and stir constantly for 1–2 minutes. The nuts will brown quickly. Do not let them get too dark. As soon as the nuts are golden brown, remove from heat and spread thin onto a baking sheet to cool. Break the caramelized nuts into small pieces when they have cooled completely.

  Yield: 2 cups

Caramelized Onions

3–4 tablespoons olive oil or whole unsalted butter
1 large yellow onion
1 teaspoon salt

Peel the onion and slice it. Cut it in half first, then slice it lengthwise (about ¼ inch). Melt the butter or heat the oil in a skillet over a low medium heat and place the sliced onion in the skillet.

  Sprinkle salt over the onions. This will help draw out some of the moisture which will prevent the onions from burning and sticking. The heat should remain at a low to medium level and just keep tossing the onion or using a spoon to stir them. It is not necessary to use sugar to caramelize onions, they have plenty of their own. Long, slow cooking will draw out those sugars and caramelize them.

  Continue to cook them until you achieve the darkness you desire. Too dark will result in a slightly bitter final product. These may be made in advance and held for one week. Remember to wrap them well to keep out other flavors.

"There is no love sincerer than the love of food."
—George Bernard Shaw

Drunken Chicken

Grilling outdoors is a "man thing." Every man thinks he can grill better than anyone else. I am no exception. I take pride in my steaks from the grill just as a golfer takes pride in his handicap or a fisherman takes pride in his catch.

Any woman will tell you that when it comes to cooking with fire, men haven't changed since the prehistoric era. If you get a pack of men together at a deer camp, the testosterone will rise to the top, and through the process of natural barbeque selection, they will determine which of the knuckle-dragging cavemen is the Master Griller.

The Master Griller is the one to whom the other Neanderthals defer. He takes care of the grilling needs of the tribe. They are the hunter-gatherers, he is the Master Griller.

Recently, *TV Guide* advertised a movie called *The Legend of Drunken Master*. I haven't seen it, but I bet it is about a bunch of good ol' Mississippi deer camp troglodytes cooking drunken chicken.

For those of you unfamiliar with drunken chicken, allow me to familiarize you with this dish and its cooking procedure. First, the tribe's Master Griller starts with a whole chicken and a full case of tall boy beer. No light beer, boutique beer, imports, or dark beer, just good old American-made beer, in the can, the cheaper the better. The Master Griller then forgets about the chicken and drinks twenty-three-and-a-half of the tall boys.

Now that he is in the proper frame of mind, the Master Griller places the remaining half of the final beer, can and all, up the chicken's butt. What the chicken did in a previous life to deserve an Old Milwaukee enema is a mystery to me. The chicken is then greased and seasoned with whatever spices are lying around the deer camp; due to the Master Griller's blurred vision they are normally the ones that are the easiest to reach in the cabinet—salt, marjoram, a ten-year old bottle of cloves, a solid clump of cinnamon. It doesn't matter. Next, the chicken is placed butt-side down on the grill. The can helps it stand up. The Master Griller then passes out.

When the Master Griller comes to, he pulls the chicken off the grill and starts drinking again. To be a true drunken chicken cooker, the cook must always be drunker than the chicken. I am a teetotaler, which makes me not fully qualified to cook a drunken chicken.

Chicken in a Basket

When I was a child, we had a preacher who raised game-cocks as a carry-over from his days before the calling. He did not fight them any more but enjoyed them for their beauty. He gave me one, but I had to return it. Some things cannot be changed by love.

I have eaten drunken chicken before. Being the only sober one in the group, I was not as impressed as the rest of the gang. There is, however, something memorable about watching a chicken roast on a grill with a beer can stuck in its rump. If you are intoxicated, it must be twice as fun.

The tribesmen's eyes always seem to light up in anticipation as the Master Griller pulls the beer can out of the chicken's rump. Come and get it!

My friend and Master Griller, Billy Ralph Winghead, cooked a drunken chicken last Fourth of July. After finishing his twenty-third Schlitz tall boy, Billy Ralph forgot to pop the tab on the twenty-fourth. Unfortunately, this was the beer that was inserted into the chicken. After twenty minutes on the grill, the barley and hops reached the boiling point inside the can. A loud explosion rocked the deer camp as the chicken launched off the grill with hot Schlitz spewing from its rectum.

The chicken rocketed over the tree line of the north 40 and was found two days later in a remote section of Perry County. Three UFO sightings were reported to Stennis Space Center as a result of Billy Ralph's drunken chicken launch. One of the Winghead boys even made it onto an edition of *Hard Copy*.

A word to the wise—when driving through Perry County, Mississippi, always beware of UFDC's (Unidentified Flying Drunken Chickens).

Roasted Peppers

Red Pepper Coulis

There are a few ways of achieving a roasted pepper. First, always use whole peppers. They are easier to work with and will cook down so much. The end result is much better if you use whole peppers.

Place the pepper on an open gas or wood grill, turning it as it gets black. If you have a gas stove at home, you can place it directly on a high burning flame, using tongs to turn it. A gas broiler on high heat will work if you get the peppers very close to the flame. Hold the pepper with tongs and slowly blacken the whole outside of the pepper.

Place the peppers into a large mixing bowl, or any container you can seal off with plastic. Tightly cover the bowl with plastic wrap. The peppers trapped in the covered bowl create steam, and the steam pushes the burnt skins away from the flesh of the pepper. This won't take long, but let them stay in there until they are cool enough for you to handle. Next, you need to peel the peppers. After the peels are removed, split the pepper and remove any seed. They are now ready for any use. Roasted peppers will hold in the refrigerator for 3–4 days as is, or for weeks if completely submerged in oil.

1 teaspoon extra virgin olive oil
⅓ cup red onion, diced
4 roasted garlic cloves
3 **Roasted Red Bell Peppers (see left)**
1 teaspoon salt
1 teaspoon black pepper
½ teaspoon whole thyme
1⅓ cups white wine
3 tablespoons heavy cream

In a small saucepan, heat oil over medium heat and add onions. Cook 3–4 minutes until they become soft and translucent (do not brown). Add roasted garlic, red peppers, salt, pepper, and thyme. Stirring well, cook 4–5 minutes. Add white wine and bring to a boil. Turn down heat, and allow to simmer 6–10 minutes. Wine should reduce by half. Remove from heat and purée, using a food processor or a blender. After the mixture is puréed, place it back into the sauce pot and place over medium heat. Add the heavy cream and simmer 4–5 more minutes.

Life is too short to stuff a mushroom."—Shirley Conran

Pizza Crusts

2 packages active dry yeast
1 teaspoon sugar
2 teaspoons honey
1½ cups warm water
5½ cups all-purpose flour
1 tablespoon salt
¼ cup olive oil + olive oil for brushing the pizza dough

Dissolve yeast, sugar, and honey in warm water.

Using a mixer with a dough hook attachment, place flour and salt in bowl and mix thoroughly. On low speed, slowly drizzle in oil and continue to mix until evenly distributed. Next, add dissolved yeast. Add remaining cup of water. Once the dough begins to come together, continue kneading it on low speed for 5 minutes. Transfer the dough onto a floured surface and work it by hand for 3–4 more minutes. The dough should now be smooth and slightly firm and dry. Place the dough in a large bowl, cover it with a damp towel, and place it in a warm place to rise for ½ hour.

Divide the dough into 6 6-ounce sections. On a dry surface, work each individual ball by rotating it in a circular motion, continually tucking the sides down and under. Form dough into a smooth ball with no air pockets. Place the balls on slightly oiled baking sheet and cover for 30 minutes. This may be done 1–2 days in advance. Dough balls can be covered tightly with plastic and kept in refrigerator.

Preheat oven to 525° and insert pizza stone. If you do not have a pizza stone, a heavy duty baking sheet will do. To stretch the dough, sprinkle a smooth surface with flour or cornmeal and flatten the dough to about 2 inches thick. Then begin gently pulling the sides and rotating the dough in a circular motion, slowly stretching it. You should be able to stretch the dough to a 7-inch diameter. Lightly brush with oil and place dough on
pizza stone. Bake for 8–9 minutes, or until golden brown. Remove and cool. The crusts are now ready to use for any recipe. Cooked pizza crust may be frozen. Pizza dough can also be cooked on a well-oiled grill.

Yield: 6 7-inch crusts

Seasoned Flour

2 cups all-purpose flour
2 tablespoons Crescent City Creole Seasoning

Mix flour and seasoning thoroughly.
  Yield: 2 cups

Clarified Butter

Place 3–4 pounds of butter in a heavy 2-quart saucepan over medium heat. Adjust the heat as butter melts so that it is bubbling. As the butter cooks, skim the white matter that comes to the top with a spoon and discard. Continue to cook butter; as it gets closer to being done the bubbles will get smaller and the butter will become clear. When the butter has very tiny bubbles and you can see through it, remove it from the heat. Allow to cool for about 1 hour and then slowly pour it through a fine mesh strainer or cheesecloth. Discard any water or solids left at the bottom.

Eggwash

Eggwash can be made by adding 1 egg to ¼ cup milk and beating thoroughly. When making eggwash for any recipe, a general rule is 1 egg per 2 portions. Most of the recipes in this book are created to serve 6 people, so generally when eggwash if referred to in this book, you will be using 3 eggs and ¾ cup milk.

Tomato Concasse

Using a paring knife, remove the core from each tomato and cut a very shallow X on the bottom of each tomato.

In a large sauce pot, bring 3–4 quarts of water to a boil. Have a large bowl of iced water ready. Place 2–3 tomatoes in the rapidly boiling water, 1 at a time. Count to 10, 15 if your water did not come right back to a boil, and pull them out using a large slotted spoon. Place them directly into the ice water. As soon as the tomatoes cool down, remove them from the ice water. Using a paring knife, remove the skin.

Cut the tomato in half horizontally and very gently squeeze out all the seeds. Dice the tomato.

Tomato concasse may be made 1–2 days in advance. Cover well as tomatoes tend to absorb refrigerator odors easily.
  Yield: 2 cups

"New Orleans food is as delicious as the less criminal forms of sin."—Mark Twain

Sauces and Stocks

Hollandaise Sauce

Crescent City Grill Creole Sauce

Tarragon Reduction
for Bernaise Sauce

Choron Sauce

Beurre Blanc

Pesto

Creole Cream Sauce

Parmesan Cream Sauce

Stir-Fry Sauce

Etouffée Stock

Seafood Remoulade

Comeback Sauce

Basil Tapenade

Ginger-Soy Butter Sauce

Spring Roll Sauce

Lemon Meuniere

Aunt Tina's Dressing

Creamy Balsamic Dressing

Raspberry Vinaigrette

A Few Notes about Stock

Chicken Stock

Veal Stock

Shrimp Stock

Gus Stop

The California Sandwich Shop and Gus's Number 2 Cafe are next to train crossings. Within walking distance of the tracks, they served passengers after long rides.

Hollandaise Sauce

"Noncooks think it's silly to invest two hours' work in two minutes' enjoyment; but if cooking is evanescent, so is the ballet."—Julia Child

6 egg yolks
¼ cup fresh lemon juice
¼ cup white wine
1 teaspoon salt
1½ cups **Clarified Butter (p. 107)**, warm but not too hot
1 tablespoon Crescent City Grill Cayenne and Garlic Sauce

Place egg yolks, juice, wine, and salt in a medium mixing bowl. Using a wire whip mix the ingredients well. Over a double boiler on medium heat, whip the yolk mixture constantly until the yolks thicken. Be careful not to scramble the eggs during the process. The yolks will be ready when you can see "ribbons" as you pull the whip through the mixture. Remove from the double boiler and slowly begin to drizzle in the warm butter while continuing to stir vigorously. If the sauce starts to become too thick, you can use small amounts of warm water to thin it down, no more than 1–2 tablespoons at a time. Once all of the butter has been incorporated, stir in the cayenne and garlic sauce. Hold in a warm but not hot area until ready to use.

Yield: 2 cups

Crescent City Grill Creole Sauce

½ stick butter
1 cup yellow onion, medium dice
1 cup green bell peppers, medium dice
3 stalks celery, medium dice
1 tablespoon garlic, minced
1 bay leaf
2 tablespoons Crescent City Creole Seasoning
1 tablespoon paprika
3 cups tomatoes, diced, juice reserved and used
2 cups V-8
1 tablespoon Worcestershire
2 tablespoons Crescent City Grill Hot Sauce
2 tablespoons cornstarch
3 tablespoons cold water

Melt butter and add onion, celery, and bell pepper; sweat 7–10 minutes until tender. Add garlic and seasoning, and cook for another 4–5 minutes. Add tomatoes and V–8 and bring to a simmer. Add Worcestershire and hot sauce. Simmer for another 10 minutes. Dissolve cornstarch in water and add to simmering sauce. Bring back to simmer and immediately remove from heat.

Yield: 2 quarts

Tarragon Reduction for Bernaise Sauce

Choron Sauce

2 tablespoons dry tarragon
1 tablespoon shallots, chopped
1 tablespoon garlic, minced
1 teaspoon black pepper
¼ cup red wine vinegar
¼ cup white wine vinegar
¼ cup white wine

In a small skillet place all ingredients over a medium low heat and cook until all liquid has evaporated. This mixture may be made and held refrigerated for 1–2 weeks. Stir ¼ cup tarragon reduction into 1 recipe of **Hollandaise Sauce (p. 110)** to make Bernaise sauce.

Purée ¾ cup of the puréed **Crescent City Grill Creole Sauce (p. 110)** and reduce it over a medium heat in a small skillet. Reduce by half. Allow to cool slightly and add to **Bernaise Sauce (see left)** to make Choron sauce.

"The greatest animal in creation, the animal who cooks."—Douglas Jerrold

Beurre Blanc

½ cup shallots, finely chopped
1 tablespoon garlic, minced
⅔ cup white wine
⅔ cup white vinegar
¼ cup whipping cream
1 pound unsalted butter, cut into small cubes, then chilled
1 teaspoon salt

In a small saucepan over medium heat, reduce wine, vinegar, shallots, and garlic. When almost all liquid has evaporated, add cream. Allow cream to cook for 1 minute. Reduce heat slightly and incorporate the butter. Add only a few pieces at a time. Stir constantly using a wire whisk until butter is completely melted and then add a few more. When you have incorporated all of the butter, remove from heat. Strain and hold in a warm (not hot) area until needed.

Yield: 2 cups

Beurre Blanc variations:
(all added after sauce is finished and strained)

Creole Beurre Rouge—Incorporate ¾ cup puréed **Crescent City Grill Creole Sauce (p. 110)** to 1 batch of beurre blanc.

Tarragon and Chive Butter Sauce—Add 2 tablespoons tarragon reduction and ¼ cup fresh chives just before serving.

Tomato and Basil Butter Sauce—Add ½ cup fresh **Tomato Concassee (p. 107)** and ⅓ cup freshly made **Pesto (p.113)** just before serving.

Roasted Garlic and Red Pepper Butter Sauce—Add ¼ cup roasted garlic purée and ½ cup finely diced **Roasted Red Peppers (p. 105)**.

Wild Mushroom and Rosemary Butter Sauce—Add ½ cup finely minced sautéed shiitake (or another flavorful mushroom) and 1 tablespoon fresh chopped rosemary.

Dill Beurre Blanc—Stir in ¼ cup fresh chopped dill.

Pesto

½ bunch parsley leaves, stems removed
1 pound bunch basil leaves, stems removed
1 cup Parmesan cheese, grated, good quality
8 cloves garlic, minced
1 cup pinenuts, chopped
1 cup extra virgin olive oil

Place all ingredients except olive oil in a food processor. Process until smooth. With machine running, slowly add oil. Turn off the processor and scrape down the sides. Continue to process until you have a smooth paste. Refrigerate until needed, up to 1 week. Pesto freezes well.

Yield: 2½ cups

Creole Cream Sauce

2 cups heavy cream
1 tablespoon Crescent City Grill Creole Seasoning
2 tablespoons Worcestershire sauce
2 tablespoons Crescent City Grill Hot Sauce
1 teaspoon paprika

Place all ingredients in a double boiler over medium high heat and reduce by one-third until thickened.

"Cooking is like love, it should be entered into with abandon or not at all"
—Harriet van Horne

My South

Thirty years ago I visited my first cousin in Virginia. While hanging out with his friends, the discussion turned to popular movies of the day. When I offered my two-cents on the authenticity and social relevance of the movie *Billy Jack*, one of the boys asked, in all seriousness, "Do you guys have movie theaters down there?" To which I replied, "Yep, and we wear shoes, too."

Just three years ago, my wife and I were attending a food and wine seminar in Aspen, Colorado. We were seated with two couples from Las Vegas. One of the Glitter Gulch gals was amazed, amused and downright rude when I described our restaurant as a fine-dining restaurant. "Mississippi doesn't have fine-dining restaurants!" she demanded, as she snickered and nudged her companion. I fought back the strong desire to mention that she lived in the land that invented the ninety-nine-cents breakfast buffet, but resisted. I wanted badly to defend my state and my restaurant with a fifteen-minute soliloquy and public relations rant that would surely change her mind. It was at that precise moment that I was hit with a blinding jolt of enlightenment, and in a moment of complete and absolute clarity it dawned on me—my South is the best-kept secret in the country. Why would I try and win this woman over? She might move down here.

I am always amused by Hollywood's interpretation of the South. We are still, on occasion, depicted as a collective group of sweaty, stupid, backwards-minded, and racist rednecks. The South of movies and TV, the Hollywood South, is not my South.

My South is full of honest, hard-working people.

My South is colorblind. In my South, we don't put a premium on pigment. No one cares whether you are black, white, red, or green with orange polka dots.

My South is the birthplace of blues and jazz and rock-and-roll. It has banjo pickers and fiddle players, but it also has B. B. King, Muddy Waters, the Allman Brothers, Emmylou Harris, and Elvis.

My South is hot.

My South smells of newly mown grass.

My South was the South of *The Partridge Family, Hawaii 5-0,* and kick the can.

My South was creek swimming, cane-pole fishing, and bird hunting.

In my South, football is king, and the Southeastern Conference is the kingdom.

My South is home to the most beautiful women on the planet.

In my South, soul food and country cooking are the same thing.

My South is full of fig preserves, cornbread, butter beans, fried chicken, grits, and catfish.

In my South we eat foie gras, caviar, and truffles.

In my South, our transistor radios introduced us to the Beatles and the Rolling Stones at the same time they were introduced to the rest of the country.

In my South, grandmothers cook a big lunch every Sunday.

In my South, family matters, deeply.

My South is boiled shrimp, blackberry cobbler, peach ice cream, banana pudding, and oatmeal cream pies.

In my South people put peanuts in bottles of Coca-Cola and hot sauce on almost everything.

In my South the tea is iced, and almost as sweet as the women.

My South has air-conditioning.

My South is camellias, azaleas, wisteria, and hydrangeas.

My South is humid.

In my South, the only person who has to sit on the back of the bus is the last person that got on the bus.

In my South, people still say "yes, ma'am," "no, ma'am," "please," and "thank you."

In my South, we all wear shoes—most of the time.

My South is the best-kept secret in the country. Please keep the secret—it keeps the jerks out.

Parmesan Cream Sauce

1 quart heavy cream
½ pound Parmesan cheese, grated
⅓ pound Romano cheese, grated
2 teaspoons white pepper
⅛ teaspoon nutmeg
light blond roux—3 tablespoons butter + 4 tablespoons flour

Bring heavy cream to a boil. Add cheese and stir well. Add pepper and nutmeg. Separately, make a light blond roux. Add roux to the milk/cheese mixture and continue cooling until thickened.

   Yield: 1 quart

Stir-Fry Sauce

½ cup soy sauce
2 teaspoons sesame oil
1 tablespoon Worcestershire
1 tablespoon fish sauce*
½ cup **Chicken Stock (p. 126)**
½ cup sherry
¼ cup white wine
1 tablespoon garlic, minced
2 teaspoons ginger, minced

Combine the first 5 ingredients in a small saucepan and bring to a low simmer. In a separate saucepan, bring the sherry to a boil and immediately remove from the heat. Add sherry, ginger, and garlic to the other simmering ingredients and remove from heat. Let ginger and garlic steep for 1 hour and strain through a fine mesh strainer. This sauce may be made in advance and held in the refrigerator for 1 week.

   * Available in oriental specialty markets.
   Yield: 2 cups

"The true cook is the perfect blend, the only perfect blend, of artist and philosopher. He knows his worth: he holds in his palm the happiness of mankind, the welfare of generations yet unborn."
—Norman Douglas

Etouffée Stock

Seafood Remoulade

"Half the cookbooks tell you how to cook the food and the other half tell you how to avoid eating it."—Andy Rooney

1 cup butter
1 cup yellow onion, small dice
½ cup celery, small dice
½ cup green bell peppers, small dice
½ cup red bell peppers, small dice
3 tablespoons garlic, minced
1 bay leaf
1½ cups flour
2 tablespoons paprika
3 quarts hot **Shrimp Stock (p. 127)**
½ cup fresh tomato, medium dice
½ cup tomato sauce
¼ cup sherry
1 cup green onion, chopped
½ cup fresh parsley, chopped
⅓ cup Louisiana Hot Sauce
1 tablespoon Old Bay Seasoning
1 tablespoon Crescent City Grill Creole Seasoning
2 teaspoons salt

In a large saucepan, melt butter over medium heat. Place the onions, celery, peppers, garlic, and bay leaf in the melted butter. Cook for 6–7 minutes, until vegetables become soft. Add flour and paprika to the vegetable mixture to make a roux. Cook roux until light brown. Slowly whisk in hot shrimp stock and bring to a low simmer. Adjust heat if necessary to keep mixture at a slow simmer for 30 minutes. Add sherry after 30 minutes and continue to simmer 10 more minutes. Add the remaining ingredients and remove from heat. Sauce may be made several days in advance and held in the refrigerator until needed.

Yield: 1 gallon

1 large stalk celery
½ medium-size onion
1 cup ketchup
3 tablespoons fresh lemon juice
¼ cup prepared horseradish
1 cup mayonnaise
3 tablespoons Crescent City Grill Creole Seasoning
2 teaspoons Lawry's Seasoned Salt
1 teaspoon garlic, minced

Chop onion and celery in the food processor until it is small but not completely puréed. Place onion and celery into a mixing bowl. Add remaining ingredients and mix well. This sauce can be made and held for up to 1 week before using. Best if made at least 1 day in advance.

Yield: 1 quart

Comeback Sauce

1 cup mayonnaise
½ cup ketchup
½ cup chili sauce
½ cup cottonseed oil
½ cup yellow onion, grated
3 tablespoons lemon juice
2 tablespoons garlic, minced
1 tablespoon paprika
1 tablespoon water
1 tablespoon Worcestershire
1 teaspoon pepper
½ teaspoon dry mustard
1 teaspoon salt

Combine all ingredients in a food processor and mix well.
   Yield: 3½ cups

Basil Tapenade

1 cup black olives
1½ ounces anchovies, drained and patted dry
1 teaspoon Dijon mustard
2 tablespoons capers
2 tablespoons freshly squeezed lemon juice
2 tablespoons brandy
3 tablespoons olive oil
½ teaspoon black pepper
1 cup **Pesto (p. 113)**
½ of 10-ounce can Rotel tomatoes, drained

Process the first 6 ingredients in a food processor until the mixture begins to get smooth. Slowly add olive oil and garlic. Add pesto and tomatoes, and pulse until all ingredients are incorporated into a smooth, spreadable sauce. May be made and stored in refrigerator for up to 1 week.
   Yield: 3 cups

"No man under forty can be dignified with the title of gourmet."—Brillat-Savarin

Ginger-Soy Butter Sauce

"There are three species of creatures who when they seem coming are going, when they seem going they come: diplomats, women, and crabs."—John Hay

2 cups orange juice
½ cup rice wine vinegar
½ cup white wine
1 tablespoon garlic, minced
1 tablespoon shallot, minced
1 orange, cut into slices
2 tablespoons fresh ginger, chopped (it is not necessary to peel)
1 jalapeño, rough chop
¼ cup whipping cream
1½ cups unsalted butter, cut into cubes and then chilled
2 tablespoons soy sauce

In a medium saucepan, place the first 8 ingredients over medium heat and reduce to reach a thick syrup. Watch it closely; mixture burns easily. Lower heat and add cream. Bring the mixture back to a simmer. Start adding butter, stirring constantly. Add more butter as it dissolves until all butter is incorporated. Strain sauce through a fine mesh strainer and finish with soy sauce.

Yield: 2 cups

Spring Roll Sauce

1 fresh jalapeño, seeded and chopped
6 tablespoons granulated sugar
1 7¼-ounce jar Hoisin sauce (best quality)
¼ cup cold water
2 teaspoons garlic, minced
juice of ½ lime

In a food processor, purée the jalapeño and the sugar. Transfer sugar mixture to a mixing bowl. Add remaining ingredients and stir well. Allow to sit for 1 hour stirring frequently.

Yield: 1½ cups

Small Change

The Mayflower diner in downtown Jackson still uses the original condiment stand, and fresh flowers make the seafood even fresher.

Lemon Meuniere

Aunt Tina's Dressing

"The primary requisite for
writing well about food is a
good appetite."
—A. J. Liebling

1 cup **Veal Stock (p. 126)**
1 cup white wine
¼ cup lemon juice
1 pound unsalted butter, cut into chips

In a small saucepan heat the veal stock, white wine, and
lemon juice. Reduce by half. Turn off heat and whisk in cool
butter chips.
  Yield: 1½ cups

⅓ cup tarragon vinegar
4 tablespoons apple cider vinegar
2 teaspoons black pepper
1 tablespoon paprika
2 teaspoons salt
⅓ cup bleu cheese crumbles
2 teaspoons garlic, minced
1 cup cottonseed oil

Mix all ingredients together. Store in an airtight container.
Shake well before serving.
  Yield: 2 cups

Creamy Balsamic Dressing

3 egg yolks
2 eggs
½ teaspoon dry mustard
2 tablespoons garlic, minced
½ teaspoon white pepper
1 teaspoon garlic salt
⅛ teaspoon cayenne pepper
2 tablespoons parsley, chopped
2 teaspoons oregano, dried
2 tablespoons red wine vinegar
¼ cup balsamic vinegar
1 cup ranch dressing, prepared
1 cup cottonseed oil
1½ teaspoons salt

Combine all ingredients in the bowl of a food processor except ranch dressing and oil. Mix well. With the machine running, slowly drizzle in ranch dressing and then cottonseed oil. Refrigerate until ready to use. This dressing will hold 1 week refrigerated.

Yield: 3 cups

Raspberry Vinaigrette

3 cups raspberries, frozen
½ cup sugar
1 tablespoon lemon juice
2 teaspoons Dijon mustard
1 tablespoon shallots, minced
1 teaspoon thyme, freshly chopped
¼ cup raspberry vinegar (if you cannot find raspberry, balsamic vinegar will do)
¼ cup cider vinegar
2 tablespoons lemon juice
2 cups cottonseed oil
½ teaspoon black pepper
1 teaspoon salt

In a small sauce pot, cook raspberries with sugar and 1 table-spoon of lemon juice until tender. Purée and strain with a fine mesh strainer to remove seeds. Add all other ingredients except the oil to the raspberry purée and beat with a wire whip. Slowly add oil while continuing to whip dressing. Recipe may be made and stored for up to 1 week in refrigerator.

Yield: 3 cups

"There is a communion of more than our bodies when bread is broken and wine drunk. And that is my answer, when people ask me: Why do you write about hunger, and not wars or love?"
—M. F. K. Fisher

A Few Notes about Stock

There are a million different variations of stock recipes out there and invariably, what you end up doing is figuring out just how you like your stocks and broths to taste by adjusting any certain ingredient. There are some key factors you should know, however, to ensure you always have a clean, sweet tasting stock.

First, and I feel most important, is to *never* let your stock boil. When a stock boils, it agitates the bones, which are loaded with calcium. Calcium released into the stock will have two effects: first of all, it will be cloudy. Second, your final product will be slightly bitter, not such a big deal if you are using it as is, but if you are going to reduce it down to make a sauce, the bitter flavor will become concentrated. Stirring the stock has the same effect as boiling. However, tempting it is to stir a big pot, leave this one alone, and make sure the other curious by-passers do too.

Next, some people brown bones for stock and other people don't. Browning the bones gives you a nice, dark caramelized stock—very sweet in flavor. Stocks made from browned bones have much less body, so reducing them to make any kind of sauce requires much more stock to make the same amount of sauce. If you are going to make soups or sauces which require a roux, browned bones are more appropriate. Just be careful not to burn them while browning them.

Always start with cold water. Hot water seals the bones and doesn't allow all that good flavor and gelatin to release.

If you have problems finding bones in the grocery store, find a good local butcher. He should have some around or will save some for you if you ask. Chicken bones are probably the hardest to find, wings work well and are not too expensive. You can also save any carcasses you have from buying whole chickens and freeze them until you have enough.

Beef bones can substituted for veal bones, but if you have to do this, use 75 percent beef bones and 25 percent pork bones. Beef bones tend to be bitter; the pork bones help to soften the flavor.

All stocks freeze well. Make lots and freeze in containers that can be used as needed.

"The secret of staying young is to live honestly, eat slowly, and lie about your age."
—Lucille Ball

**Bigger
than a Bread Box**

The image of the Sunbeam girl no longer adorns the sides of delivery vans. This is one of the few left on the back lot of the EarthGrains Company which owns the name.

Chicken Stock

Veal Stock

4 pounds chicken bones
1 gallon cold water
1 pound yellow onion, cut into large pieces
¾ pound carrots, peeled and cut into large pieces
½ pound celery, cleaned and cut into large pieces
3 bay leaves
½ bunch fresh parsley
4–6 sprigs fresh thyme
3 garlic cloves, peeled and smashed
½ tablespoon cracked black peppercorns

Rinse the chicken bones under cold water for 4–5 minutes. Place the bones in a large stockpot, and cover them with the gallon of cold water. Place over low medium heat and *slowly* begin to bring to a simmer. Using a ladle, skim off any gray foam that floats to the top and allow stock to come to a very slow simmer with tiny little bubbles gently rising to the surface. Once you have achieved this temperature, and you feel you have skimmed most of the foam, set a timer for 2 hours and walk away. At the end of the 2 hours, skim the stock. There may be a good bit of fat floating. Add the vegetables. If the stock has reduced, add another 1–2 cups of water. This should not be necessary if you have cooked it slowly. Once again, set the timer, this time for 5 hours. Periodically, check it to make sure the heat is keeping the stock at a steady slow simmer. When the timer goes off, turn the heat off and get a large strainer. Strain the stock and discard all bones and vegetables. Fill sink with heavily iced water and place the container of stock in the ice bath to cool as quickly as possible. Once stock is completely cooled, remove any fat from the surface.

Yield: 3 quarts

4 pounds veal bones
1 gallon water
1 pound yellow onion, cut into large pieces
¾ pound carrots, peeled and cut into large pieces
½ pound celery, cleaned and cut into large pieces
3 bay leaves
½ bunch fresh parsley
4–6 sprigs of fresh thyme
3 peeled garlic cloves, smashed
½ tablespoon cracked black peppercorns

Rinse the veal bones under cold water for 4–5 minutes. Place the bones in a large stockpot, and cover them with the gallon of cold water. Place over low medium heat and *slowly* bring to a simmer. Using a ladle, skim off any gray foam that floats to the top and allow stock to come to a very slow simmer with tiny little bubbles gently rising to the surface. Once you have achieved this temperature, and you feel you have skimmed most of the foam, set a timer for 6 hours and walk away. Keep an eye on it as you will be adding more water to this stock as it cooks. After 6 hours, skim the stock to remove fat and scum, and then add the remaining ingredients. Top off the stock with water again and let it cook for 12–14 hours. (In restaurants, veal stocks are cooked 24–36 hours.) Periodically, check it to make sure the heat is keeping the stock at a steady slow simmer. When the timer goes off, turn the heat off and get a large strainer. Strain the stock and discard all bones and vegetables. Fill sink with heavily iced water and place the container of stock in the ice bath to cool as quickly as possible. Once stock is completely cooled, remove any fat from the surface.

Yield: 3 quarts

Shrimp Stock

2 pounds shrimp heads and shells, rinsed well and dried
½ cup cottonseed oil
½ pound yellow onion, peeled and medium dice
⅓ pound carrots, peeled and sliced thin
⅓ pound celery, cleaned and sliced thin
⅓ cup tomato paste
1 cup white wine
2 bay leaves
¼ bunch fresh parsley
4–6 sprigs thyme
1 tablespoon cracked black pepper
2 cloves garlic, crushed
1 gallon cold water

Preheat oven to 400°. Dry the shrimp shells as much as possible to prevent splattering.

Place oil in the largest ovenproof skillet in your kitchen and turn the heat to high (You may set off your smoke alarm making this stock, but that's okay.) Put the shrimp shells in the oil and just let them sit for 1–2 minutes (stirring will cool down the skillet). The shells should turn a coral-pink-brown color. Stir 2 or 3 times until all shells have achieved this color. Turn the heat down to medium and add the vegetables. Cook for 6–10 minutes, stirring occasionally. Add the tomato paste and stir it in to coat the vegetables. Place this mixture in the oven for 10 minutes. Remove from the oven and place all ingredients into a large stockpot. Deglaze the skillet with the wine. Add this to the stockpot. Cover the mixture with cold water. Add the fresh herbs and bring up to a medium simmer. You do not want to boil out of control, though. Cook for 2–3 hours—you'll have to taste it to decide if it is done. If you are able to use a lot of shrimp heads, and not just shells, you will achieve a more intensely flavored stock even quicker. Strain and cool as with the other stocks.

Yield: 3 quarts

"I did toy with the idea of doing a cookbook. . . . I think a lot of people who hate literature but love fried eggs would buy it if the price was right."
—Groucho Marx

Desserts

White Chocolate Bread Pudding

Chocolate Decadence

Chocolate Volcano

Pumpkin Cheesecake

Pumpkin Raisin Muffins

Watermelon Sorbet

Strawberry Shortcakes

Caramel Custard

Peach-Blueberry Ice Cream

Crescent City Grill Bread Pudding

Blueberry Crème Brulee

Lemon Crepes

**Have Your Cake
and Eat It too**

I always wanted the corner
piece with the flower.
Working after hours, a local
eatery allowed me to capture
this cake rack before a
new curved glass model
replaced it.

White Chocolate Bread Pudding

5 ounces white chocolate

4 egg yolks

1 egg

¼ cup sugar

2 teaspoons vanilla extract

1½ cups heavy whipping cream

½ cup milk

¼ teaspoon salt

1 large loaf of French bread as needed (crusts cut off and cut into 1-inch cubes)

Melt white chocolate in a double boiler. In another double boiler over moderate heat, combine eggs, sugar, vanilla, whipping cream, milk, and salt. When blended and warm, add melted chocolate and stir well. Fold bread cubes into custard mixture. Let it sit for 5 minutes and then mix on low speed in an electric mixer using the paddle attachment. Pour into a buttered 2.2-quart Pyrex baking dish and cover with parchment paper. Bake at 350° for 45 minutes. Remove paper and cook an additional 15 minutes to brown the top. White Chocolate Bread Pudding can be held in the refrigerator for 2 or 3 days. When cooled completely, scoop out individual portions and heat to just warm in a microwave. Top with the warmed white chocolate sauce.

White Chocolate Sauce

8 ounces white chocolate

½ cup heavy whipping cream

Melt white chocolate in a double boiler. Add heavy cream and blend thoroughly. This sauce will hold in the refrigerator and can be reheated in the microwave until just warm.

Yield: 8–12 servings

Chocolate Decadence

Brownie Crust

4 squares Baker's Semisweet Chocolate (4 ounces)
¾ cup butter, salted
4 eggs
1½ cups sugar
1 cup flour
1 teaspoon vanilla extract
1 cup chopped pecans
pinch of salt

Preheat oven to 325°. Melt the chocolate and butter together over a double boiler. In a large bowl, cream sugar and eggs together. Slowly add the chocolate mixture. Add the remaining ingredients, but do not over-mix. Line a 10 x 16-inch cookie sheet with wax paper. Pour batter onto cookie sheet, making sure it is evenly distributed. Place in preheated oven. Bake for 30–35 minutes or until a toothpick comes out clean. Allow to cool for 5 minutes; then turn brownie cake out onto a clean, dry surface and allow it to cool a bit more until it is cool enough that you can handle it.

Using the bottom circle of a 10-inch springform pan, cut a springform-pan-sized circle towards one end of the brownie cake. Next assemble the springform pan and lock into place. Place the round brownie cake circle in the bottom of the springform pan, and then cut the rest of the brownie into strips to line the sides of the springform pan forming a brownie crust on the bottom and sides of the pan. You will probably end up with some odd size pieces, but the cake is moist enough that you can press them together for a solid crust. Let the crust chill while you make the mousse recipe.

Chocolate Mousse Filling

3 pounds Baker's semisweet chocolate, chopped fine (may substitute chocolate chips)
¾ cup strong brewed coffee or espresso
2 tablespoons Taster's Choice crystals, dissolved in ¼ cup hot water
¾ cup egg yolks
¾ cup egg whites
¼ cup sugar
2 cups heavy whipping cream

Combine the chocolate, coffee, and Taster's Choice in a double boiler and heat until the chocolate is melted. In a large mixing bowl, beat egg yolks slightly and slowly add the melted chocolate being careful not to cook the eggs. Set chocolate mixture aside.

Thoroughly clean and dry a separate mixing bowl and a whip attachment for an electric mixer. It is important when whipping egg whites that all utensils be very clean. Place egg whites in the clean bowl and begin to whip on high speed of an electric mixer. When they begin to become foamy, slowly add in sugar and beat until stiff. Set egg whites aside. In a separate bowl beat whipping cream until it has doubled in volume.

Fold ⅓ of the stiff egg whites into the chocolate mixture and mix gently. Add remaining egg whites. Once the egg whites are incorporated, use the same technique to fold the whipped cream into the chocolate. Pour the mousse mixture into the brownie-lined springform pan. Place in the refrigerator.

It will take about 8–10 hours for the mousse to set up. This cake is best when made a day in advance. Once set, cover tightly with plastic wrap to avoid absorbing refrigerator odors. To serve, use a hot, damp knife and cut into 12–16 portions.

Yield: 12–16 servings

"Conversation is the enemy of good wine and food."
—Alfred Hitchcock

Chocolate Volcano

"Forget love. . . I'd rather fall in chocolate!" —Unknown

1½ cups butter, unsalted
10 ounces chocolate, chips or block cut into small pieces
4 eggs
4 egg yolks
¾ cup flour
1½ cups powdered sugar
raspberries, fresh

Preheat oven to 375°. Over a double boiler, melt butter and chocolate and mix well. Using a wire whip of an electric mixer, incorporate the eggs and yolks 1 at a time. Add flour and powdered sugar and beat until smooth.

Lightly flour and butter ovenproof 6-ounce gelatin molds. Fill mold halfway with batter and place 2 raspberries in the center. Fill molds with batter, leaving ¼ inch from the top unfilled, and bake for 12 minutes. Allow the molds to sit for 2–3 minutes, then carefully unmold them onto serving dishes.

Yield: 6–8 servings

Do You Know the Muffin Man?

Halloween is associated with the glow of jack-o-lanterns. Still one of my favorite holidays, it's a time when a kid can be a kid or a ghost or a vampire or a princess or. . . .

Pumpkin Cheesecake

Crust

3 cups graham cracker crumbs
⅓ pound butter, melted
½ cup sugar
⅛ teaspoon nutmeg
¼ teaspoon cinnamon

Combine all ingredients and press crust along the bottom and up the sides of a springform mold. Refrigerate until filling is ready.

Filling

2 pounds cream cheese, softened
¾ cup sugar
¾ cup brown sugar
4 eggs
4 egg yolks
1 12-ounce can pumpkin pie filling
1 tablespoon vanilla
½ cup whipping cream
1 teaspoon cinnamon
½ teaspoon nutmeg

Preheat oven to 300°. In a mixer, using the whip attachment, combine cream cheese and sugars and whip until smooth. Add eggs 1 at a time until completely incorporated. Add pumpkin, vanilla, and spices and beat until smooth. Turn mixer to low speed and add cream. Mix until cream is incorporated. Pour cream cheese filling into springform mold and bake for 1 hour, 30 minutes. The cheesecake should jiggle just slightly when done. Refrigerate for 24 hours. Use a hot, wet knife when cutting to get nice, smooth pieces.

Yield: 12–16 servings

Pumpkin Raisin Muffins

4½ cups flour
3 tablespoons baking powder
1½ cups sugar
1½ cups brown sugar
1½ teaspoons salt
2 teaspoons nutmeg
2 teaspoons cinnamon
2 eggs
3 cups buttermilk
½ cup melted butter
1 cup pecans
1 15-ounce can pumpkin
2 cups raisins

Preheat oven to 400°. Combine flour, baking powder, sugars, salt, nutmeg, and cinnamon together and mix thoroughly. In a separate bowl, mix eggs, buttermilk, and melted butter. Fold liquid ingredients into dry ingredients. Do not over-stir. Add pecans, pumpkin, and raisins. Pour muffin batter into greased muffin tins and bake for 30 minutes or until a toothpick inserted in the center comes out clean.

Yield: 2½–3 dozen

Watermelon Sorbet

2 cups water
1 cup sugar
3 cups watermelon purée

Dissolve sugar in water. Add watermelon purée. Freeze in an ice cream maker using the manufacturer's instructions. To check the correct levels for simple syrup to purée, drop a clean whole egg into the mix. The portion of the egg that rises out of the mixture should be the size of a quarter. Adjust the water-to-purée ratio to make the egg rise or drop in the mix.

Yield: 6 1-cup servings

Strawberry Shortcakes

3½ cups flour
½ tablespoon baking powder
¼ teaspoon baking soda
½ cup sugar, plus ¼ cup for sprinkling
¾ cup unsalted butter, cold
2 eggs
⅔ cup milk
¼ cup unsalted butter, melted

Preheat oven to 375°. In a mixing bowl, combine flour, baking powder, baking soda, and sugar. Cut in cold butter and mix until there are no large pieces. Beat eggs and milk together and mix them into flour mixture. Do not over mix. Place dough on a lightly floured surface and roll it out to 1½-inch thickness. With a 3-inch cookie cutter, cut biscuits and place them on a baking sheet. Brush the tops with melted butter and sprinkle sugar over them. Bake for 25 minutes or until golden. To check doneness, insert a toothpick into center. It should come out clean. Allow to cool slightly before topping.

Topping

2 pints fresh strawberries, cleaned and sliced
1 cup sugar
¼ cup lemon juice
1 cup whipping cream
1 teaspoon vanilla
¼ cup powdered sugar

Combine berries with sugar and lemon juice and allow to sit for 2–3 hours in refrigerator.

Whip cream in with vanilla and powdered sugar until it holds a peak. Top biscuits with berries and a dollop of freshly whipped cream.

Yield: 8–10 servings

Caramel Custard

1 cup sugar
⅓ cup water
5 eggs
⅓ cup sugar
1 tablespoon vanilla extract
¾ teaspoon salt
3 cups milk

Preheat oven to 350°. In a casserole dish, arrange 8 ovenproof 12-ounce bouillon bowls. In a saucepan over medium heat, caramelize sugar with water (do not stir). When sugar has reached a light caramel color, remove immediately from the heat and pour equal portions of caramelized sugar into each bouillon bowl.

In a mixing bowl, combine the eggs, sugar, vanilla extract, and salt; whisk until all yolks are broken. Scald milk and slowly whisk into egg mixture. Ladle equal amounts into bouillon bowls. Fill casserole dish with enough hot water to cover halfway up the sides of the bouillon bowls. Cover with parchment paper. Cook 30 minutes, rotating the whole casserole dish 180° at the 15-minute mark. Allow to cool completely before refrigerating. Refrigerate at least 12 hours

Using a paring knife, "rim" the bouillon bowl and turn upside down onto a chilled salad plate. Allow the cold caramelized sauce to pour out over the custard. A small amount of hardened caramel will remain in the bottom of the bowl; leave it there. Top custard with a small dollop of whipped cream and toasted almond slivers. Garnish with fresh mint.

Yield: 8 servings

"Ice cream is exquisite. What a pity it isn't illegal."—Voltaire

Stealing Watermelons

Whenever I eat watermelon, I remember my high school days, and the Great Watermelon Heist.

It was the summer of 1977. *Rocky* was in movie theaters, and "Hotel California" was on the radio. I was fifteen years old and working nights as a radio station disc jockey on the 7 p.m.-to-midnight shift. During the day I was on the summer cleaning crew at my high school. The school was small and located on the outskirts of Hattiesburg, adjacent to a farm owned by the Duff family.

I was a member of a high school fraternity. One of my coworkers on the cleaning crew was a pledge in the fraternity. This pledge (I will call him Billy Nolan) did most of the work on the cleaning crew that summer. We ordered him around a lot. "Pledge Nolan, wax the floors. Pledge Nolan mow the grass. Pledge Nolan, fire up the incinerator."

Billy Nolan was new to our school. He wanted desperately to fit in and he did all of our bidding, without complaint. Billy also owned a late 1960s model Volkswagen Beetle that we would "borrow" at least once a day to go trail riding in the woods that led to the Duff farm.

After lunch one day I ordered pledge Nolan to steal a watermelon out of the Duff family watermelon patch. I drove his beat up Volkswagen down the trail that led to the watermelon patch on the Duff farm. For the first time all summer Billy was hesitant to carry out one of our orders. He never would have thought to steal a watermelon on his own. Unfortunately, his desire to fit in overruled his good judgment, and he did as he was told.

I parked the Volkswagen on the trail, and sent him out into the watermelon patch. He crept halfway into the patch and held one up. It looked good, but I couldn't let him get off that easy. "Not big enough," I yelled. He crept a little farther out and held up a larger one. "Bigger," I said. He sneaked all the way to the other side of the field and held up one of the largest watermelons I had ever seen, one that was surely big enough to win first prize at any county fair. "Perfect," I said. On his way back to the car, I ordered, "Get two." Billy looked at me as if to say, this isn't worth it, but he picked up a second watermelon nonetheless and began the long trudge across the watermelon patch.

It was at that moment we heard, "Hey! What are you doing!" It was coming from the Duff house. It was Kenny Duff, Jr. We were caught.

"Run!" I yelled to Billy.

As he ran towards the Volkswagen, I heard the loud roar of a motorcycle in the distance. It was coming toward us. From across the field I could hear Billy yelling at me as he ran through the watermelon patch. He was letting out a high-pitched guttural scream that sounded like a wounded animal. He looked like he was running the ropes at football practice. His knees were reaching high in the air as he tried to dodge the remaining watermelons in the patch. As it turns out, he was about as good at watermelon dodging as he was running the ropes, and he was smashing a good number of the Duff's remaining melons with every other awkward step. When I saw the motorcycle at the head of the jeep trail, I took off—without Billy.

I will never forget looking in the rearview mirror and seeing Billy Nolan, eyes as big as saucers, his tennis shoes covered with watermelon pulp, running behind me on the jeep trail. To his credit, he was still holding onto both watermelons. Kenny Duff was hot on his trail.

The look in Billy's eyes was one of surprise, bewilderment, and betrayal, all at once. He was hollering for me to stop the car. His car. I kept going. I don't know how fast he was running, but I had the getaway car in third gear.

A slightly overweight fraternity pledge is no match for a motorcycle, and Billy fell to the ground, landing on and smashing both watermelons. He was also in a world of trouble. Kenny was not only the owner of the watermelon patch; he was the president of the fraternity, and there was a pledge meeting that night. Billy never told anyone who was driving the car.

After the Great Watermelon Heist of 1977, I quit my job at the school and focused on my budding radio career. I never again took anything that belonged to someone else. After his brief stint in watermelon patch enforcement, Kenny Duff became a successful radiologist.

I lost track of Billy Nolan after high school. He moved off, probably up North where watermelons don't grow. If I saw him today I would apologize to him, and let him know, whether he knew it or not, he always fit in. And in the end, he had been a much bigger man, than I. He had faced the music.

Food has such strong connections with my memory. Like music, food transports me to the times and places of my youth. Every time I eat watermelon, I think of Billy Nolan and how he was a better friend to me than I ever was to him.

Peach-Blueberry Ice Cream

2 cups sugar

pinch of salt

5 cups milk

4 eggs

3 egg yolks

2 teaspoons vanilla

14 ounces sweetened condensed milk

1 cup whipping cream

3 cups fresh peaches, peeled, large dice

¾ cup sugar

¼ cup Peach Schnapps

2 cups blueberries, fresh or frozen

¼ cup sugar

1 tablespoon lemon juice

Combine 2 cups of sugar, salt, vanilla, and milk in a sauce pot and bring to a simmer. Remove from heat. In a mixing bowl, beat eggs and yolks together, slowly adding hot milk mixture to eggs. Place bowl over a double boiler and cook until mixture begins to thicken. Remove from heat and add condensed milk and cream. Chill.

In 2 separate skillets, you will cook the 2 fruit mixtures. Combine the peaches with the Schnapps and ¾ cup sugar and simmer until a thick syrup forms. Add to the cooling ice cream base and continue to chill. Cook the blueberries with ¼ cup sugar and lemon juice until a thick syrup forms. Chill separately.

Place cold ice cream base in ice cream machine and process until it is almost frozen. To prevent all of the ice cream from turning blue, scoop out some ice cream into container and sprinkle in some of the berries. Continue to do so until all berries are added to ice cream. Freeze for 2–4 hours and serve.

Yield: 1 gallon

Crescent City Grill Bread Pudding

½ cup butter

1 cup sugar

5 eggs

2 cups heavy cream

1 tablespoon pure vanilla extract

1 teaspoon ground cinnamon

½ cup raisins

2 loaves French bread (crusts cut off and cut into cubes)

Cream butter and sugar; add eggs, heavy cream, vanilla, and cinnamon. Place the liquid mixture and half of the bread into the bowl of an electric mixer and begin mixing on the slowest speed. As bread begins to break up, add more bread to the bowl until the mixture becomes like a damp (not too wet) mush. Add raisins and place pudding into a greased 3-quart Pyrex dish. Bake covered at 350° for 30 minutes. Uncover and bake another 30 minutes until a toothpick stuck into the center comes out clean.

Jack Daniel's Sauce for Bread Pudding

1 cup heavy cream

1 cup sugar

¼ teaspoon cinnamon

1 tablespoon butter

1 tablespoon cornstarch

2 tablespoons water

2 tablespoons Jack Daniel's

Bring cream, sugar, cinnamon, and butter to a boil and stir until sugar dissolves. Separately, dissolve the cornstarch and water. Add the cornstarch mixture to the heated sauce and stir well. Bring to a boil. Remove from heat. Add the Jack Daniels.

Yield: 8–10 servings

"Progress in civilization has been accompanied by progress in cookery."—Fannie Farmer

Blueberry Crème Brulee

"Come quickly, I am tasting the stars!"—Dom Perignon, at the moment he discovered champagne

10 egg yolks
1 cup sugar
2 cups whipping cream
2 cups Half-n-Half
2 teaspoons vanilla
3 tablespoons Grand Marnier
1 pint fresh blueberries

Preheat oven to 275°. In a large mixing bowl, combine the yolks and half of the sugar. In a sauce pot, combine cream, Half-n-Half, and the other half of the sugar. Whip yolk well while bringing the cream mixture up to a boil. Once cream mixture has come to a boil, slowly add it to the yolks. Add only small amounts at first, being careful not to scramble the eggs. Once all the cream has been added, stir in vanilla and Grand Marnier. Allow mixture to sit for about 10 minutes and then using a ladle, gently remove the foam and bubbles from the top and discard them. Place brulee dishes on a baking sheet with high enough edges that you will be able to cook them in a water bath. Divide the berries into the brulee dishes and gently ladle the mix on top. Fill the dishes up as high as possible. This will make it easier to caramelize the sugar before serving. Place the baking sheet with custard dishes on the oven rack and fill it with hot water to rim of baking sheet. Bake for 30 minutes. The custard should jiggle slightly when done. Carefully remove from the oven and then remove from the water bath. Allow to cool for 4–6 hours before serving.

To caramelize sugar:

1 cup brown sugar
blow torch

To dry the sugar, lay it out on the wax paper in a baking sheet and place it in an oven set at 100°. Stir it occasionally. Allow sugar to stay in oven for 2–3 hours. Then, let it cool and place it in the food processor and process until it is a fine powder. If you live in a dryer climate, simply spreading sugar out on a baking sheet and letting it sit out for a few days will achieve the same result.

Sprinkle the tops of the cold brulees with the fine sugar. Using a torch sweep the flame back and forth over the sugar until it browns, and serve. Be careful, caramelizing sugar will cause very bad burns. Leave the brulees on a flat surface while browning them to prevent hurting yourself.

Yield: 8–10 servings

Lemon Crepes

Crepe Batter

1 tablespoon sugar
1 cup flour, sifted
⅛ teaspoon salt
1 cup milk
½ cup water
2 eggs
1 egg yolk
5 tablespoons unsalted butter, melted
1 teaspoon vanilla
Clarified Butter (p. 107) or non stick spray for cooking crepes

In a large mixing bowl, combine dry ingredients. In another mixing bowl, whisk together wet ingredients. Add the wet to the dry and mix thoroughly. Refrigerate for 1 hour before making crepes. Heat a 6–7-inch nonstick pan over a medium high heat. Spray the pan completely, or coat surface with clarified butter. Ladle 1½ ounces of batter into the hot pan and rotate the pan so that the batter forms a sheet across the entire surface of the pan. Cook for 1–3 minutes, until crepe becomes golden brown, and flip the crepe over. Cook for an additional 30 seconds and remove crepe. Place on a flat, dry surface to cool. Repeat process until batter is gone. Layer crepes between pieces of wax paper. Makes 12–14 crepes.

Crepe Filling

1½ pounds cream cheese, softened at room temperature
¾ cup sugar
2 tablespoons finely grated lemon zest
2 tablespoons fresh lemon juice
2 teaspoons vanilla extract

Combine all ingredients and blend until smooth. Preheat oven to 325°. Fill the crepes by placing the cream cheese mixture in a pastry bag and piping a 1 x 1-inch tube down the center of each crepe. Roll the crepes and place them on a lightly buttered baking sheet, nonstick is preferable. Cover crepes with a sheet of wax paper and then cover the entire baking sheet with aluminum foil. Bake for 6–7 minutes until center is warm. While crepes are baking, make the sauce.

Sauce

½ pound butter, unsalted
½ cup sugar
¼ cup brandy
2 tablespoons freshly squeezed lemon juice

In a medium skillet, melt butter over medium high heat. Add sugar and cook until dissolved. Do not burn. Add brandy and lemon juice and mix well. Lower heat slightly and cook for 4–5 minutes, until thick and creamy. Place warm crepes on serving dishes and spoon sauce over them. Garnish with fresh raspberries and mint.

Yield: 6–8 servings

"A gourmet who thinks of calories is like a tart, who looks at her watch."—James Beard

Index

Cheaper by the Dozen

The design of donuts was created to hook them out of the hot oil that they are cooked in. Coincidently, the donut hole was invented around the same time.